540

THE SPIRIT-RIDDEN KONDE

AN ITINERANT ENTERTAINER.

He is dressed in skin and feather head-dress, armlets, skin kilt, and body rings, the number of which latter indicates his social position. He carries, as professional properties, a spear, a skin pack, rattles, horns, bells, and a stringed musical instrument.

THE SPIRIT-RIDDEN KONDE

A RECORD OF THE INTERESTING BUT STEADILY VANISHING
CUSTOMS & IDEAS GATHERED DURING TWENTY-FOUR
YEARS' RESIDENCE AMONGST THESE SHY INHABI-
TANTS OF THE LAKE NYASA REGION, FROM
WITCH-DOCTORS, DIVINERS, HUNTERS,
FISHERS & EVERY NATIVE
SOURCE

BY

D. R. MACKENZIE, F.R.G.S.

WITH MANY ILLUSTRATIONS
& A MAP

PHILADELPHIA
J. B. LIPPINCOTT COMPANY
1925

TO

MY WIFE

Preface

THIS book is not an attempt to depict the daily life of the Konde people; it rather aims at indicating, so far as an outsider can, the leading ideas and practices which make up the background, leaving to others the task of bringing the foreground into proper relief. And, after many years' residence and work among the Konde, I feel increasingly how much the fact of being a foreigner among them limits one's understanding of the people whose ideas he attempts to set down on paper. The task has been undertaken largely at the request of some of the leading men of the tribe, who are alive to the fact that the old days are passing, even among the conservative Konde, and that, if a record is to be made at all, it must be made without delay.

There is no one to whom I must acknowledge indebtedness to the same extent as I must, and now do, to native chiefs and common people, educated and otherwise; to doctors, diviners, hunters, fishers; every kind of native in fact, from whom I have caught hints, in sudden and unintentional flashes of revelation, or in sustained conversation, of what is in the Bantu mind. And therefore I have, in most chapters, aimed at using language which indicates the native attitude to the various beliefs dealt with; an attitude in most cases of unquestioning faith.

The photographs I owe almost entirely to others : to Major J. Stuart Wells, C.B.E., lately of the Tanganyika Civil Service; Capt. Perkins, 1st King's African Rifles, and Mr. E. C. Richards, Administrative Officer, and the Rev. M. H. Faulds, of Isoko. To the Rev. D. M. Brown, M.D., of Itete, I am indebted for the map which accompanies the book.

I have again and again drawn upon my wife's knowledge of the people, especially of the women and children, and to her suggestions I owe very much. By permission of the Editor of the *Expository Times* use has been made of part of the material of an article on " Christianity and the African Mind " which I contributed to that magazine some years ago.

D. R. MacKenzie.

Kyimbila, Tanganyika Territory,
   February, 1925.

Contents

xiii

Contents

List of Illustrations

xvi List of Illustrations

The Spirit-Ridden Konde

CHAPTER I

The Land & the People

UNGONDE, as the Konde people call their country, lies around the north end of Lake Nyasa. Northwards of that point it stretches for about fifty miles, and southwards for roughly the same distance. Like all their neighbours, the Konde belong to the great Bantu race, which occupies Africa from the Cape to the Congo, and beyond.

The lake shore plain is narrow, fertile, and populous, with its centre at Karonga, where there is a British Magistrate, some trading stores, and a station of the Livingstonia Mission of the United Free Church of Scotland. Beyond the plain the tribe, under various local names, reaches up into the mountains on both sides of the lake. Outside of Nyasaland, and northwards across the Songwe, it covers a large area in what was once German East Africa, but is now known as Tanganyika Territory. Here, too, the plain is hot, fertile, and populous as at Karonga. Northwards of the plain lie the healthy uplands of Mwamba and

Bukukwe, culminating, so far as the peopled regions are concerned, in Tukuyu, five thousand feet above sea-level, the residence of the Administrative Officer and his staff, with Post and Telegraph Offices, and a large Government Hospital. Here also are many small trading stores, conducted by Indians and Somali; and a little to the south is the Kyimbila Station of the Scottish Churches Mission, carrying on the work of the exiled German missionaries. Still further to the south, and less elevated, is the British military post of Masoko.

The population of these fertile and healthy highlands is dense. From Tukuyu or Kyimbila, looking south and west, numerous villages, each hidden in its banana grove, fill the view westwards to the Bundali Hills, where the Kibira River is marked out by a morning mist, and southwards towards the lake, thirty miles distant. In this region the people call themselves Nyakyusa, with a number of local names indicating no difference of origin or language. The soil is so fertile, and the rain usually so abundant, that in many places two crops are taken annually of some foodstuffs, while of the others the single crop is so great that scarcity, no uncommon occurrence in some parts of Central Africa, is rarely experienced.

The Bundali Hills close in this happy valley (for in spite of its elevation the country has the appearance of a valley) on the west; and beyond them, after a most exhausting march, over lofty summits, through deep ravines threaded by bridgeless rivers, one comes to the home of the Bandali, a race of hardy highlanders closely related to the Konde. Here, at Isoko, is another station of the Scottish Churches Mission.

Eastwards of the Tukuyu uplands lie the Kinga Mountains, better known as the Livingstone Range, near the foot of which lies the Itete Station of the Scottish Churches Mission. From here one gets a view of lake and mountain, river and plain, which may well be regarded as one of the finest of the kind in Africa. The evening sun, shining upon the great mountain mass, reveals hundreds of crevices and folds in which lie tiny houses, beside waterfalls or rapidly dashing streams ; while up to the summits stretch the wheat-fields, green or golden yellow in the evening light. At one's feet sleep the countless villages, banana hidden ; and away in the distance Lake Nyasa reflects the last gleams of departing day.

Over the mountains lies the country of the Kinga people, a land indescribably rough and mountainous, but here and there well watered, with fertile valleys producing wheat, oats, peas, in abundance, besides the usual African products. Here the cold is so great that during part of the year many of the people sleep in pits hollowed out of the ground, and heated by fires which are extinguished at bed-time.

Northwards the upland valley is bounded by the Igale Hills, from the top of which one looks to the lofty Mbeye Mountain, which from one point of view presents an astonishing likeness to Arthur's Seat and the Salisbury Crags at Edinburgh. Beyond Igale live the Sango and the Safwa, the former a vigorous and warlike tribe, the latter until recently their oppressed subjects and slaves.

The earliest traditions go back to a time when the Konde dwelt in Malongo, in the area now known as Mahenge. There their god Ngeketo, roused to wrath by three attempts to destroy him, abandoned them, and is now the God of the white men. Whether on this account, or for some other reason, a great migration brought them to the country north of the Songwe River, where they settled down, no doubt conquering older inhabitants. At some unknown time, but before the Angoni reached so far north in their great march from Zululand, the Sango, neighbours of the Konde northwards, were driven out of their homes by intertribal warfare. They broke down over the intervening mountains, and overcame the unwarlike Konde, among whom they settled down as chiefs, retaining until now the tradition of their Sango ancestry. Whether at the same or another time, the Kinga, probably for the same reason—pressure from behind—swarmed down the steep mountain passes, and established themselves in the Nserya region.

One of the leading Kinga chiefs was Mwangonde, who, under the name of Chungu, occupied land at Kabari, near the Mwakeleli Mission Station. His son, Kyabara Chungu, setting out with an armed force in search of more fertile garden land, met with varying fortunes, until he was finally obliged to cross the Songwe into what later became Nyasaland. In this region Chungu seems to have made easy con-

quests. He passed through the mountain region
north and west of Karonga, receiving the submission
of the chiefs as he went; thence he descended into
the plain at Karonga, finally establishing himself at
Mpande, where his descendants still live.

The legends which have gathered around the
person of Chungu reveal him as a man of impressive
personality. One legend states that having established himself at Karonga, he cast longing eyes on the
regions on the other side of Lake Nyasa. With a
great following he went down to the lake, smote the
water with his sceptre, and crossed on dry land.
Receiving the submission of the people, he returned
as he went; followed later, but in canoes, by a great
multitude of people, who wished to settle under the
shadow of so great a chief. The European attitude
towards this event is shared by native Christians, but
quite intelligent pagans meet scepticism, quietly and
gravely, with the statement that " Chungu is the man
who speaks with God." The incident, or whatever
event it represents in its present form, can only be
satisfactorily accounted for by regarding it as what
the Higher Critics call a " later accretion "; for the
Angoni, with their own story of a similar crossing of
the Zambesi, had not yet arrived, the Arabs were
still in the distance, and direct Christian influence
did not begin for many years afterwards.

It is needless to give in detail the history of his
successors. One lost much land to rival chiefs;
another was deposed because he could not give rain
in a time of drought. The country fell into confusion·

Prophets arose who foretold the coming of the Angoni and the Arabs to work havoc on land and people. Then from the lake would come the strange white man who would overcome Angoni and Arab, and give peace to the land. To this race the people were directed to submit themselves when they came. So deep and sure would the peace be, that men would go armed only with sticks, all need for spear and shield having passed away.

But the peace was still in the future. Arab and Angoni came and fulfilled their destiny. The Henga or Kamanga people, fleeing before the latter, were received by the Konde, and were at first friendly to their hosts, but later, when the Arabs arrived as traders and slavers, made an alliance with them against the harassed Konde. Into this confusion entered, very dramatically, the white man, of whose coming the natives give graphic accounts. The approach of the *Ilala*, the tiny steamer of the Livingstonia Mission, then operating from Cape Maclear, far to the south, struck the people with terror. " It is God," they said, " He walks on the water." As the little vessel drew near the land, the people fled into the bush. A white man landed. A few strong-hearted natives ventured to approach, and saw his white skin. " It is surely God," they said, " He has come to us in the likeness of men." When he ate some bananas in their presence, they said, " No, not God, but a friend of His."

In 1887 the African Lakes Corporation of Glasgow

opened a trading store at Karonga, under Mr. Monteith Fotheringham, a man of great vigour and capacity. His presence aroused the hostility of the Arabs, who feared the loss of their slaving profits, and a period of fighting followed, in which the Konde took sides with the white man as their one hope. After a great encounter with their enemies, the defeated Konde took refuge in the Kambwe lagoon, the dry reeds on the margin of which were set on fire by the victors. The helpless natives leaped into the water, where many were drowned, and numbers were taken by the crocodiles which swarmed in the lagoon. In 1895 a small force was moved up by Sir Harry Johnston, High Commissioner for the newly formed British Protectorate, and the Arabs were defeated, and their leader, Mlozi, hanged the same day. From that time the Konde have progressed in peace under the influence of Government, Trade, and Missions.

One incident, very striking in itself, may be given as indicating the influence of Chungu. On one of her trips the *Domira*, the steamer of the African Lakes Corporation, went ashore on the sands near Karonga. Vigorous but unsuccessful efforts were made, with the help of great gangs of natives, to float her ; and at length Chungu was asked to lend his powerful aid. This was Chungu Mwakasungula II. Taking with him a white cock, he went with his councillors to where the stranded steamer lay helpless on the sand. The following prayer, which he offered, was given to me by the son of one of the councillors who stood near him :

"Art Thou angry with me, O God, who didst redeem me from slavery? The Angoni mocked me, the Arabs mocked me; then didst Thou cause me to see these mighty ones (the Europeans); and I said, 'Rejoice, for God has heard my prayers.' Who, then, of my ancestors is angry? Against whom have I sinned? For it is they who are my helpers in speaking to Thee. Many of them died by the spear; they saw their families destroyed; they suffered hunger again and again, before the mighty ones came. Now, O God, be merciful, and let the feet of these men come up out of the water."

Then taking water in his mouth he squirted it north and south saying, "I am lord of that country, I Magemo: I am lord of that country, I Kyabara," to which the assembled councillors responded, "E! Magemo; E! Kyabara." Then whirling the cock over his head and dipping it in the water, he gave the signal to the men hanging on the ropes to pull. And the steamer floated off into the water!

Meantime in the north internal warfare went on intermittently, but no man of outstanding capacity arose to give cohesion to the various families of the Nyakyusa. Before the arrival of the Moravian missionaries in the area in 1891, various Europeans visited the district. Hunters came and went, and for a brief space there was a station of the Livingstonia Mission not far from Tukuyu. In 1893 the German

Government established a station at Lumbira on the lake shore, but removed later to Tukuyu. On the whole the new Government was well received. A rising in 1897 was so mercilessly dealt with that any discontent which might be felt was suppressed by the fear of the German machine-guns. Very slowly the district is being merged in the general progress arising out of European domination.

Around the lake shore cotton is being successfully cultivated by natives and Europeans. On the uplands near Tukuyu there are some coffee plantations, and the suitability of the soil for the cultivation of flax is being tested. Coal has been found in the hills to the west, but its commercial value has still to be proved; and a small quantity of mica is also being digged. Up in the north, on the Lupa River, but outside the Konde region, gold has been discovered, but apparently only in modest quantities. There are at present about three score of miners at work there.

CHAPTER II

Village Life

THE typical Konde village has very little in common with a European one. Here and there one will come on villages neatly laid out in streets or rows, usually with the ends, rather than the sides, facing the road; frequently with a clump of bananas separating one house from another. But much more common is the village in which each house is hidden in its own banana grove; or where at one point one may find three or four huts grouped together, at another perhaps a solitary hut, yonder, again, two or three are near each other; but everywhere surrounded by bananas growing close up to the houses. Or, in a few places, the tall maize conceals the houses from view in the growing season, leaving them exposed, after the harvest, to the eye of all passers-by.

From a distance nothing is seen but the wide spreading banana leaves. In the early morning from hundreds of huts smoke rises into the still air, as the sleepers rouse themselves and lay fresh wood on the fire which has been smouldering all night, unless some one has wakened and stirred the dying embers. One by one the villagers emerge from the houses, and

26

sit in the sun, greeting neighbours with a polite
" Have you slept well ? " if there are any neighbours
near. Then the husband milks the cattle, and the
boys come to drive them out to the pasture, where
they will remain until the early afternoon, when they
are again milked.

Generally the cattle sleep in the same house as their
owners, tied up to stakes fixed deep in the floor ; but
where there are grown-up sons not yet married, a
separate house is built in which the parents sleep with
the little ones, while the young men guard the cattle
from raiding thieves.

The bed is frequently no more than a mat spread
on the mud floor, with a single blanket for covering,
and no pillow, unless it is a piece of roughly trimmed
wood. The more prosperous natives, earning good
pay in the employment of Europeans, have well-made
beds fully equipped, in many cases even with mosquito
nets hung from the roof. The poorer consider that
they have made a great step forward if they have
been able to save up enough money to buy a single
blanket, and not seldom even that belongs to the
father, the mother and children having to be content
with meagre coverings of calico or grass mats. But
the house is warm, often too warm, for the fire is
always burning, the door is closed, there are no
windows, and there is no ventilation in the roof ;
and all the inmates sleep with their feet to the fire,
which is in the middle of the floor.

Here and there one will come upon rows of tiny
houses, each built and occupied by two or three small

boys, who have grown too big to occupy any longer the single-roomed hut in which their parents dwell. They are slender erections of reed and grass, and look as if a strong wind might carry them away ; but the children live a happy, and not always innocent, life in these huts until they are able to build bigger ones for themselves.

Dress is more conspicuous by its absence than by its presence. During the day the women wear little but a long strip of bark cloth hanging down almost to the ground before and behind. The children usually have nothing at all, unless they have the good fortune to get a strip of cloth from a grandparent. They go about quite naked for the first few years of life, and a mission school usually reveals rows of children who consist of long legs and arms and smiling faces, wholly unconscious of need if they have a tiny rag strung in front, often not more than a few square inches in size. But the men who are earning money may be well dressed. The richer wear trousers and jacket, a shirt, a collar and tie, boots, if they are able to afford them, and a helmet. Their wives and children wear long robes of highly coloured cloths, and are no doubt observed with envy by their less fortunate sister-women, with little but a piece of bark-cloth to hide their nakedness. The average man, however, goes to church or market with a single garment, unsewn, flung over his shoulders, and covering, more or less completely, his whole body ; but he goes to work in a scanty waist cloth, which leaves him un-covered below the knees and above the waist. Men of social position are known by the number of *manyeta* (body rings worn on the waist) which they wear : one for a man or woman just " above the common " ; six or seven for a man of high standing. A few women have begun, to their own great discomfort, to wear the immense coils of brass or iron on wrists or ankles which are so popular among other tribes.

Clothes, says an acknowledged authority on the subject, make the man. Not among the Konde. Chungu is a great chief, but his greatness does not depend on what he wears, although there are occasions when he dresses more carefully than at other times. This almost naked man is regarded with a reverence greater than is granted to any but a very few Europeans, and out of all recognition greater than is felt for the native who swaggers about in boots and helmet and white man's clothes. The respect which is accorded to a European depends to-day (though it did not in the past) upon his personal character, his control of resources, the authority which has been bestowed upon him by others. But Chungu, with hundreds of other chiefs throughout Bantu Africa, has a respect which is gained in a totally different fashion. He is in close touch with unseen powers. His prayers have a compelling power, his benediction is priestly, his curse of fearful validity. He is a channel through which may come weal or woe upon the land ; and hence his authority depends in no degree upon such an accident as dress.

By almost all who know them the Konde are re- garded as lazy. And to the bustling, and perhaps

unobservant European, village life affords abundant
justification for the charge ; while even the most
observant and sympathetic must admit that they are,
to put it mildly, a people with a large amount of
unimproved leisure on their hands.   There is, in
truth, a good deal of idle lounging in the sun, and it
is thoroughly enjoyed ; and so long as it remains
unproved that the restless energy of the white man
has succeeded in securing the best possible conditions
for the great masses of his race, just so long will
some white men, and a vast majority of black,
decline to admit that the African is altogether on
the wrong path, and the European altogether on
the right.

   If the year has been a good one, the father has very
little care upon his shoulders : his barns are well
filled, and hunger is not likely to trouble him and his
family ; his children are healthy, and perhaps doing
well at the little mission school ; he has paid his tax,
and the precious certificate, signed by the magistrate,
is carefully laid away in some place of safety ; his
house is re-thatched, and will keep out the rain ; his
cattle and sheep and goats are away with the village
herd, and looked after as part of the village property.
If he wants a little money for immediate use, he can
go to the nearest white man with a sheep or a goat
for sale, or perhaps his wife will go with fowls or eggs,
or a bunch of bananas.   Finally, if he is religiously
inclined, whether he is a Christian or not, he has
probably been to church on Sunday, a fact which
adds to his sense of personal well-being during the

week. He has, then, no reason for doing any more work. Work has yielded him all that he requires, and he may lie in the sun and chat lazily, or move about strumming his *pango* (stringed instrument) with that supreme unconsciousness of being an idler, which is to some so irritating, to others so charming, a characteristic of the African.

All this, however, is ideal, and seldom corresponds to the actual fact. The year may have been a bad one; ill-health may have overtaken himself or his family; his cattle may be dying; or he may have failed to find employment after long trekking in search of it, and consequently his tax is unpaid and trouble is hanging over him. But a normal year, neither unusually prosperous nor unusually disastrous, will reveal how the Konde fill in their time. Let it be understood that they see nothing but folly in working for what they do not want. Working for what other people want is a high form of altruism to which only a small number of Konde have risen. That work increases the wealth of the country is a doctrine of high economics which they do not understand : wealth is increased by good harvests and by increase of live-stock.

The whole life of the community centres round the hoeing season. During the great heat which usually precedes the rains, the people move languidly about, incapable of anything like exertion. The men gather in groups and lie idly in the shade, talking languidly, droningly; an illness or a death; a marriage settlement; the wealth some one has brought from the South; or perhaps they exchange impressions of Europeans they have worked for—a subject into which a great deal of humour can be packed; for it must not be imagined that the white man is taken too seriously. His little foibles, his often none too good temper, his haste to get a job done, and above all his cool assumption of unquestioned superiority, supply endless fun to the village joker. " Bantu as she is spoke " by some Europeans gladdens the weary hours for many a humorously inclined native.

Should the rains be late, the situation may be serious, for not only does the heat continue, but the harvest will be correspondingly late, and there is dark fear lest the supplies in the barns, intended to last until March, should have to do until April is well on. Public prayer is offered, led by the chief. The preliminary ceremonies have been attended to, and as soon as the first rains fall all sally out with the first streak of dawn to begin the year's work. From a score of small crofts one may hear the long happy shout of the men, and the shrill call of the women, as they toil in the early morning; but as the day advances and the heat increases, the shouting dies away, and every one puts the last ounce of energy into the task in hand. Henceforward, for about three months, the native gives all his attention to his crops ; for as the season advances, and the grain begins to grow, the weeds come up also in wild profusion, and

A KONDE VILLAGE, LAKE SHORE TYPE.

The slender houses are of reeds and grass, shaded by overhanging banana leaves, and usually unplastered to admit every straying breeze. As cattle stealing s a very common crime, the cattle sleep in the houses with their owners,

sheer hard work makes men and women look thin and haggard. Work stops about noon ; the women go home to attend to the food, the men to see to the cattle which the smaller boys have been looking after during the day. The milking is always done by the men ; it is not women's work as with us. If there are flies about, and there usually are, the cows need no invitation to thrust their heads into the column of acrid smoke that arises from a dung fire, kindled for the purpose. The rest of the afternoon is filled either with small duties, basket mending, net work, some slight repairs to a canoe, rope making, house repairing ; or it may be there is a lawsuit to be settled, and every idler will make a point of being present.

By the time food is over, night has closed in. If the night is dark, one after another slips away with a friendly " May you sleep well," and silence reigns until morning. Unless it is suddenly broken by the roar of a lion or the growl of a leopard ; and then the young men, who sleep with the cattle, rush out with spears and clubs and wild shouting to drive off the intruder, while the others raise a weird cry within the houses. Should the lion take refuge in a thicket and refuse to be driven off, a small party may slip round to the nearest white man, if he is not too far away, to beg him either to lend them a rifle, or to come himself to their aid. In the warm moonlight nights, however, other noises fill the ear. The young people gather for a dance, and the drum fills the night air with its interminable tum tum tum, now soft and

c

low, again rising to a perfect fury of rapid sounds, not without a certain rhythm, but with rasping effect upon the nerves of Europeans tossing sleeplessly in the warm humid air.

After harvest comes the house-building ; and when that is finished the men are free to go out to seek work. They usually set out in companies, for the Konde dislikes being alone on a journey. Like all home-loving people, they are suspicious of strangers, and if they have to pass through another tribe, they take great care to guard their small possessions ; seldom more than they are wearing, and a spear or a club to guard them from the more obvious dangers of the way. There will be a few youths going out for the first time, with a wild flutter at the heart, of fear and expectancy. Fear, for they have heard strange tales of the white men and their ways ; expectancy, because of the wonderful things they will see : the great houses, steamers, trains, motors ; and what must seem countless white men to those who have been accustomed only to the missionary, the magistrate, and the storekeeper, and even these perhaps some days' journey from home. And who knows but he will come back with money in his pocket, wearing gorgeous raiment, a helmet perhaps, and, above all other things to be desired, a pair of boots ! Those who stay long come back with the spoils of civilisation ; highly coloured cloths, cheap clocks, melodeons, mouth-organs, worthless pocket-knives, which they deal out to admiring friends and acquaintances.

Life is never dull for the African. There are marriages and funerals here as elsewhere; the former always a joyous occasion, the latter not always or necessarily the reverse. A walk through a populous village will bring one upon net making, pot making, basket or cloth weaving, and one may hear the sharp tap-tap of the bark cloth worker, or, in an iron-working district, the clang of the blacksmith's stone hammer, beating out hoes or spears upon a rough stone anvil. And many drive dullness away with beer. Sometimes it is a small party. A few friends gather in a house, and sit around a pot or two of beer provided by the wife of the host. They drink to the strumming of a *pango* or the beating of a small drum, for they like to have music at their feasts, even when only a few are gathered. But if it is a village feast, given by the chief, it may go on all night with terrific noise, shouting, singing, and drumming; and not always does the feast end without fighting. 155439

Sometimes the villagers receive visitors. The native evangelist on his rounds is always hospitably welcomed. The tax collector is not exactly welcomed—who ever welcomes a tax collector?—but he is received well enough, for his coming has at least this advantage, that those who are ready to pay the sum demanded will not have to go later and pay at the *boma* (magistrate's office), which may be a long distance away. Sometimes a native trader comes along, his packs carried by attendants, for he never carries them himself, even when beginning on a small scale. Visitors of more importance are the magistrate and the missionary, whose coming is usually heralded afar, by the report that he is already in the district, and is now perhaps only a day's journey off, slowly making his way from village to village, and dealing with whatever matters require his attention as magistrate or missionary. His coming is a matter of importance, for he will have a number of men with him who will need food, by the sale of which the villagers hope to make a few honest pence; though abundance of food is often given freely as a token of welcome. As the great man approaches the village, all the younger people come out to meet him with shouts of welcome, and if he is travelling in a *machilla*, the men will take the pole from the bearers, and with tremendous noise enter the village and deposit him at the school or the chief's house.

And the sadder side? Sickness, epidemics, the perpetual fear of witchcraft and of evil dreams foreshadowing ill, theft with its ever-present possibility of accompanying murder, quarrels that will not heal, forced marriages, and all the hidden cruelty that so rarely comes to the surface. Most pathetic of all, perhaps, the feud between old and young; the young all for to-day and to-morrow, for the new ideas, the hope of progress; the old for yesterday with its stability and ordered life; the young going in crowds to church, the old going secretly, and no doubt sadly, to worship at the ancient shrines, guarding the approaches lest the levity of youth should desecrate the place of terror, and evil come upon all the land; the young gathering around the white man, and lending themselves to his purposes, the old even to-day approaching him with reluctance, if at all, for to them he still retains much of the awe and hidden power with which he was credited in the earlier days.

The individual Konde is not so popular with white men as are members of other tribes; indeed there are employers who will not knowingly give work to a Konde at all. As workmen, it must be acknowledged that they are both less active and less reliable than surrounding tribes; they are neither so intelligent nor so loyal to contract. The Konde soon wearies of effort, and longs to get back to the lowing of his cattle and his pretty little hut in its banana grove. He loves his children, and the hope of being able to clothe them if he works well, does not compensate him for prolonged absence. Loyalty, as the Henga, Angoni, and Yao are loyal, does not distinguish the Konde, who show loyalty rather to chief and to tribal custom, than to the white man with his problematical benefits. They have never attached themselves to the European, as many of the surrounding tribes have done; for the Konde are less convinced than others that the one hope of Africa is the European and his influence; less convinced, be it added, that Africa stands so desperately in need of saving. That may be due to their unawakened condition—and, again, it may not. Educationally, too, they are less advanced than other tribes. Only a few of them are to be found in Government offices, or doing the skilled work which commands such good pay from Europeans; nor have they supplied, in any numbers, the trained assistants in Mission work who form one of the principal successes of Missions among other tribes.

But this does not imply that the Konde are without virtues. They are very shy, and respectful to authority, the latter a characteristic that atones for many defects in the minds of those who consider subserviency the primary virtue in a native of Africa. Their conservative nature prevents them being too free with strangers, and they will not greet a passing European, either until he takes the initiative, or until long friendship has convinced them that it will not be regarded as an undue liberty. Once their confidence has been gained, they are found to be merry, laughing, and bright. The friendliness of children is an attractive feature of the tribe. And the adults are most willing to be friendly also, provided the first advances are made by the European. When one begins to know them intimately, it becomes obvious that their backwardness is not due to lack of capacity, but to an unyielding conservatism, which leads them to think long—and some have been thinking for a generation—before committing themselves to anything new. " We will think about it " is a common response to invitations to take their place alongside the more progressive tribes. Yet with it all they are a lovable people, responsive to friendliness, deeply attached to each other, and to all who rightly claim the name of friend.

Slavery is, formally at least, a thing of the past. It is asserted by natives that some men and women are still in slavery, but while that is not impossible, no one has ever been able, or willing, to give me the name of either slave or owner in a single case. Yet such is the terrifying influence which some natives exert over others, that it is not difficult to believe that here and there throughout the country there may be individuals to whom continued slavery is a smaller evil than the wrath of an exposed owner, and therefore the fact of their bondage is not reported to the authorities.

Many circumstances might combine to make the freeman a slave, and the slave a freeman. A man who led astray the wife of a chief, if discovered, paid a son or daughter to the husband. So also, one found stealing from a garden was similarly penalised. Mocking at a lame man was a crime which could only be atoned for by the same kind of payment; and a man who could not pay just debts might himself be taken by the creditor. Prisoners of war, it need hardly be added, were slaves. On the other hand, the owner might find himself obliged by circumstances to restore children so obtained; if not, he was obliged to find wives or husbands for them. A slave might be a member of the council, and there are cases where slaves acquitted themselves so well in battle that they were granted their freedom. So long as it remained purely domestic, it was not an altogether intolerable condition. There was an ex-slave living at Karonga not long ago, who supported as long as she lived the old woman who was once his owner, and that, as he assured me, from genuine affection. On the other hand, a man, not yet beyond the prime of life, was present when a slave was buried alive along with the body of his late owner. And another knew of a slave, bound and weighted with stones, thrown into the lake to feed the crocodiles. Such things may with reason be assumed to be impossible to-day, whether it be true or not that slavery still exists.

CHAPTER III

Konde Children

THE small Konde boy or girl stands gazing with frightened eyes at the *unsungu* (white man), and the little heart can be seen beating through the dark soft skin, while the breath comes and goes in rapid motion, and the tiny legs are ready to run at the first sign of a too near approach. For the white man is the bogey of the Konde child. From earliest infancy he has been taught to fear him, to regard him as a possible source of dreadful danger. "The white man will get you" is as common a threat as its parallel of the dreadful black man, with which foolish people at home inflict injury upon their children. The first impulse of a child in arms, approached in the most kindly fashion by a European, is to scream, and clasp its mother by the neck in an agony of fear. But once gain the confidence of these tiny black folks, and you find them as friendly, as delightful, as charming, as white children of the same age. Possibly the charming period passes sooner, for the Konde child begins to know good and evil at an age when the white man's child is still a mere prattler. Little black, or rather brown, folks are of a quick intelligence, ready to learn, full of romping glee ; and the musical jingle of the tiny bells that most of them wear on their ankles up till three or so is pleasant to the European, and rings with a thrilling response in the heart of the adoring mother, who sits on the ground watching the gambols of her little one.

The unborn child is treated with great care, and surrounded with superstitions. The mother must submit to restrictions in regard to diet, and indications of the sex of the coming child are given by the preferences she shows for permitted foods. She must not eat hot food, for that would burn the child's head ; nor beans, for they might cause the disease called *ilyulu*. An expectant mother who drinks much milk will bear a son ; if she has a great desire for flesh foods, a daughter is known to be coming. A scolding woman need not be surprised if her child is a boy, especially if her husband is the victim of her language. Some women will not eat rice, perhaps because it is a new food, all the possibilities of which have not yet been fully explored.

The worst possible place for a woman to have her child born is at her own father's house, unless it is with the consent of her husband ; for every one will assume that the child has an unknown father. If an expectant mother suspects her husband of sorcery she will take care to have her child born at a distance, so that it may not inherit its father's undesirable powers, these being transmissible only at close quarters, and only after birth. With heathen women, the birth, if in the daytime, takes place mostly in the open air, as much privacy as possible being secured in the universal banana groves : and always in a sitting, not a lying position.

A difficult birth is a serious misfortune for the mother. Births are normally easy, and difficult labour indicates the wrath of the spirits for evil done. Medicine is in all cases given to facilitate delivery, and if this fails other means must be tried. A message is sent to the husband and the father of the woman, and prayer, without ceremony, for the matter is urgent, is offered by both men :

> " Ye fathers and ancestors, and ye who are of the far past, let this child be born safely. If I have sinned, be merciful ; and if ye will not be merciful, kill me, but let the woman and the child live."

While thus praying he has been chewing the pith of a banana leaf, and at the end he takes water into his mouth, which he squirts out, saying, " Let my sin be carried away," and throws on the roof the chewed pith ; for if he is not by birth the representative of the family he has no natural right to pray, but the ceremony of chewing and throwing on the roof averts evil consequences.

If all this fails it is clear that the woman has sinned ; and her only hope of life for herself and her child lies in confession. The midwife takes a number of small sticks which she throws on the ground one by one, inviting the suffering woman to name the men with whom she has consorted. Natives assert emphatically that birth becomes easier after confession ;

and the statement cannot be altogether devoid of truth. The influence of the mind upon the body is universally admitted : may it not be that the consciousness of guilt has the effect of contracting the muscles, and the relaxation which follows confession renders birth less painful ? And may it not be that even a false confession, wrung from a despairing sufferer, brings a momentary relief sufficient to bring the child to the birth ? One is glad to add, however, that many women have the courage to refuse altogether to submit to this shameful ordeal, insisting that their trouble is due, not to the wrath of the spirits, but to other causes, and that they will die rather than confess what is not true.

When birth has taken place, the cord is cut with a bamboo knife, and the placenta buried in the family place of prayer, a small part protruding to leave a connection which insures further children. All this time no one in the house may swallow saliva. The father calls out to know the sex of the child, but he must not yet enter (for the party have entered the house as soon as possible after the birth). After a few days the mother is anointed with oil and shaved, along with her child, and powdered with medicine. Meantime intimation has been sent to the grandparents ; a cock if a boy, a hen if a girl, telling them all that they wish to know. The mother may now resume her household duties.

But in about a week she goes to show the child to her own parents, and at the end of her visit, which lasts some weeks, great preparations are made by both

sets of grandparents. The mother sets out from her
father's house with a train of friends carrying food,
and a very special friend who carries the baby. Arrived
at the paternal grandfather's, the food is laid down,
and the child is taken by the grandfather, who presents a hoe to the maternal grandmother; and then,
with the child in his arms, goes to the *ikiyinja* (the
family place of prayer). He spits into the palm of
his hand, and, laying it in blessing upon the child's
head, he prays:

" May it be well with you, my child. Ye spirits,
be not surprised at this child of yours whom I present to you. I am old: let him take my place.
Care for him in this world of sickness. I was alone,
and ye have multiplied me and made me a company.
Be not angry, but bless the child; and in the sight
of God let him be acceptable."

The mother sits with head covered, for she must
not be seen by her father-in-law. The parties now
exchange gifts of food, and eat separately, after
which the grandfather gives the child a gift, usually
now a small coin, over which the little hand is closed.
Next, the grandmother takes the infant and hands it
to its mother, who, with a pot of beer on her head,
goes off with her husband to their home. Arrived
there, but not till then, the father takes the child in
his arms, and thanks it for the gift it has brought, a
foretoken of more yet to be earned.

Lingering here and there in certain families are
strange customs, probably belated survivals from

earlier days. The family of Lugulu at Mwakeleli wear blinders of leaves for weeks after a birth. At the end of the period a feast of beer and ill-cooked food is prepared, and both sets of families spend the night in open reviling of each other, and ceaseless tramping of the feet the livelong night. In the morning good food is eaten, and both parties go their ways with mutual good will. This is called *ukutila indila*, to fear the fears ; to endure the terrors. No explanation of what the terrors are has reached me.

The birth of twins is regarded as one of the greatest of misfortunes, and is followed by ceremonies intended to cleanse the parents from the stain which has come upon them, and to prevent its spread to others. A hut is built outside the village, with a partition in the middle, on either side of which the parents live, but they must speak to each other only in whispers, and to others not at all. The doctor sprinkles all the relatives with medicine, and kindles a fire, in the smoke of which every one must stand for a moment. The parents are shut up in the hut, but may leave it for a few moments at night, and no one may see them. After about a month the doctor comes again, with beating drums and shaking rattle, and brings the parents out of their house of restraint. A second sprinkling of medicine upon each relative being made, the doctor takes a bunch of grass from the roof, kindles it, and hands it to the father, who, holding it in one hand, crawls out of the house, and runs, followed by the crowd. He returns, however, and receives their

salutations with his hand upon his mouth. Beer mixed
with medicine is handed to him, and, all the others
drinking one by one from a calabash, he takes a little
into his mouth and squirts it upon each as he or she
drinks. The final stage comes about a month later,
when, in the presence of the doctor, without whom
nothing can be done, all the grandparents and both
parents drink beer amid a circle of shouting villagers,
and then, laying hold of the calabash, break it in
pieces. After one more sprinkling of all, the doctor
departs, taking with him a cow as fee for his many
exertions. But until another child is born, the parents
must eat alone, or with other parents of twins ; and
the mother may not pass behind anyone without warning them and receiving their consent, signified by
clapping the hands.

The naming of the child. The Konde child possesses a varied selection of names. When he is grown
he will offer a European employer one or another,
sometimes in perfect honesty, sometimes with intent
to hide the fact that under a previously given name he
had a bad character. But the names are all genuine.
Descent is through the father, and the new-born child
takes the personal name of its paternal grandfather,
let us say Ambangire. But his mother must never
refer to her father-in-law by name, nor may she use
the name in referring to any other person who bears
it ; her son therefore takes her own name ; if she is
called Kalukwa, he will be named Mwakalukwa ; next he
takes the family name of his father, say Mwakasungula.

He is now Ambangire Mwakalukwa Mwakasungula;
but his mother usually has a pet name for him,
which no one else uses; and, finally, at marriage he
takes yet another name, used only by his wife. But
only one name is used at a time. When the personal
name, Ambangire, is used, he is among familiar friends;
when he is called Mwakalukwa he is being referred
to as his mother's son; and when it is desired to
honour or humour him he is given his title of
Mwakasungula.

Girls take the personal name of the paternal grandmother, but are sometimes referred to by their father's
family name.

For boys, the work of life begins at about five. It
is a greatly longed-for promotion, for at that age many
of them go out with the bigger boys to herd the village
cattle. One may see almost anywhere a couple of
infants, with long sticks, looking after herds of fifteen
to twenty head of cattle, and having a thoroughly
good time of it. In the low-lying plains they do not
begin till they are eight, for there the grass is longer,
and the ever-present dangers of the bush are more
difficult to guard against. The boys, big and little,
get together in groups, and there is no kind of evil
that growing boys can learn that they do not learn
during that period; but they learn also much that is
good, and useful in after life. About eight to ten
thousand children of all ages attend the Mission schools,
but with many attendance is spasmodic, and the great
school of life is the bush. The majority of parents
follow the educational principles of Mr. Samuel

Weller, senior, and turn their children out into the bush to learn whatever the companions they find there have to teach them.

They play at " grown-ups," having their own chiefs and headmen ; build houses, pay taxes, learn various useful and many injurious things. Their " chiefs " demand taxes, and there is no pretence about it. A boy must steal, even if it be from his own parents, whatever his chief wants, and pay it to him as tax. More serious thieving is often attempted, and the chief, who is usually the biggest bully of the crowd, will bring to trial and punishment the very boys whom he sent out to steal. Mimic battles are fought in good temper, but they sometimes end in serious injury to some of the warriors. The great achievement which all boys burn to excel in is the high leap, and a thrashing may be the portion of the unlucky one who is weakest. Tricks of many kinds are indulged in, one of the favourites being to send a mere child off on some errand, and on his return direct him to sit in a place where a fire has been kindled, and the ashes removed in his absence ; or he is ordered to sit where thorns have been placed for him. No boy dares to disobey such orders.

Mimicry is a favourite amusement. I have seen remarkably good imitations of motor-bicycles made by quite small boys, even the " phut-phut " being reproduced by another boy running along with a bent reed touching the ground. Lanterns are made out of pumpkins, as boys at home make turnip lanterns. Hats and shoes are fashioned out of leaves, and tiny

D

canoes of maize leaves are sent floating down stream, with shouting and racing competition between the owners.

Girls help their mothers, and at a very early age look after their younger brothers or sisters. It is a common sight to see a small girl staggering along under weight of a fat baby brother strapped to her back.

In the hotter regions boys go naked till ten or twelve, wearing nothing but a piece of string on the waist and a charm on neck or wrist. Girls begin to wear bark-cloth waistbands at five or six, adding more as circumstances permit. Their clothing is provided by the father ; but boys, at whatever age they begin to wear any kind of garment, have to earn it for themselves, for it is not the business of their fathers to clothe them. They often, however, get a fowl or two, or even a goat or a sheep, from a grandparent, with the proceeds of which they buy a yard or two of cloth.

In the great majority of families there is a cruel difference in the treatment of boys and girls. The boys are uncared for, dirty, unoiled, not too well fed ; while the girls are kept clean and oiled, well fed, and as far as possible clothed at an early age. The reason is not far to seek. Girls are a source of wealth, and a dirty, ill-cared-for girl will command few head of cattle when the time comes to think of her marriage. Boys, on the other hand, have value only as representatives of the family when the father has passed to the spirit world, and that value is not dependent on external circumstances. A change is being effected, however, by the fact that, in the neighbourhood of Europeans, boys can earn money, and so help the family exchequer.

Puberty is reached at about fifteen, and boys pass that stage without ceremony. Girls are segregated, usually in groups. They lie on leaves spread on the floor, and must not be seen by boys, unless they are the daughters of chiefs, who are permitted to see boys at night. The initiate receives instruction, usually from her mother, though there are plenty of willing advisers besides, in household matters. When this is over, the wife of the *mfusya* (the man who was go-between at her parents' marriage) comes, with others, to inquire about the girl's character, to which a favourable answer is given by the mother : she cooks for strangers, has never known a man, and is of good temper. Then she is examined, and if she is found to be impure (as she is ; there is practically no exception), she is put up into the rafters, where she is half-choked in the fumes of a smoky fire specially kindled. Here she remains until permitted to come down, a severe beating following upon any attempt to escape. (The cleansing power of smoke is to be noted also in connection with twins.) The children of Christian parents are examined in the same way. Happily the situation is improving, though very slowly. After being thoroughly smoked, the girl is washed and oiled, and the *banyago* (older women) come to instruct her in all her duties to husband and children when she has them.

Immediately after the initiation rites the betrothal

ceremonies begin ; indeed, the one passes into the other. Girls are sometimes betrothed before birth, but this is usually done only when a wife has died, and the father, being obliged to supply another, offers the widower the next child to be born if it is a girl. He sends a boy to the man as a guarantee of good faith, but the boy remains only a week or so, and then returns to his home.

It may be accepted as certain that no boy comes through the dangers of adolescence unharmed. Fathers are said to warn their growing sons about these dangers, and sometimes they threaten to refuse to find wives for them if the warning goes unheeded ; but nothing more is done, and the threat is never carried out.

Children's games are much too numerous for anything but a mere reference. For quiet moments, puzzles ; or guessing what is in the hand of another ; or what object, out of sight, is being touched. A favourite river- or lake-side sport is diving and staying under water while some one counts. Walking on the hands or on stilts is very popular.

Yangilo is a ball game, with sides, the ball being thrown from one to another on the same side, while the other side endeavours to get and keep it a given number of throws, without letting it fall to the ground or into the hands of the opponents. *Inguba* is a game not unlike our hockey, a ball being struck about, and kept as far as possible within one's own side. *Ngulya* is played with sides sitting at a distance from a small object set up in the middle, while any round thing is thrown at it from side to side, the winning side being the one that hits the object a given number of times in succession.

Ingaramu, the lion, is a piece of banana cord attached to a string and whirled round the head, when it makes a noise remotely resembling the growling of a lion. *Ifula,* rain, is our bull-roarer; old people still believe that it stops the rain; but even they admit that no well-disposed spirit takes any notice of child's play. *Bandu* is a kind of top, spun by twirling it between the palms and letting it go. Whip-tops are in use, but are of European origin. A kind of mimic ammunition is supplied by the seeds of the *unsyunguti* tree, which are thrown at the enemy, and all who are hit are " killed," and carried off the field.

Konde children are perfectly happy. Those who go to school hail the dismissal hour with the same shouts of joy as little people at home. The boys will climb a tree perhaps, with the more glee if the teacher's prohibition has added a whiff of danger to the exploit. Or they will chase an unfortunate goat around; though the goat, having been handled from earliest kidhood very much as we handle pet dogs, probably enjoys the sport as much as the boys do. A couple of boys may get astride a young bullock, and go careering along the road; or more likely the whole troop will make a rush for the nearest water in river or lake, and with terrific noise splash about in joyous excitement. No doubt those who are utterly unclad look with envy on the scraps of clothing worn by their more fortunate fellows, but that does not silence the shout of glee which fills the air as boys and girls are let loose from school. Where there is no school there is not the joy of being " let out " ; but other joys exist, for the Konde child is just as much an adept at finding outlets for his energy as European children are when left to themselves.

CHAPTER IV

Husband & Wife

DOES the African buy his wife? The answer must be ambiguous, because the situation is so. I put the question to two highly educated natives, and both, independently, gave an immediate and emphatic " Yes." I put it to some elderly men of no education at all in our sense of the term, and they indignantly answered " No." There are, too, educated Africans, of many tribes, who resent as an outrage the suggestion of purchase. And wives, whatever the implication may be, take pride in the number of cattle paid for them, much as a girl at home might regard with satisfaction the amount of dowry she brought to the common purse. Some years ago a bride went to her husband, with the full consent of her father, no cattle, or any other goods, having been given for her, but the experiment was disastrous. The other married women regarded her with contempt, as a person of no consideration. A most unhappy life followed, and in a very short time the home was broken up. Such an attitude, however, is obviously not permanent. The Christians of the Tonga tribe gave up, some time ago, the whole custom, with, I understand, no evil results.

No Konde youth can get a wife if he, or his family

on his behalf, cannot find the requisite number of cattle to hand over to the relatives of the bride ; but the idea of purchase is not present to the minds of any of the numerous relatives on both sides who take part in the discussion ; and in point of fact nothing corresponding to our idea of purchase takes place. The wife is in no sense a slave. She belongs to her husband only in the sense in which the wife of a white man belongs to him. The cattle are, indeed, a *quid pro quo*, for the man who has got a wife has got a good thing, and it is, say the Konde, right that the parents, who had all the trouble of bringing his wife up for him, should get some return for their toil. The father, in receiving the cattle, guarantees the conduct of his daughter in all that is expected of a wife, but in nothing that is expected of a slave. She is not a chattel, as our own laws once declared a wife to be. If she goes astray, the cattle, with the increase, are returned to the husband. On the other hand, if the husband is divorced, he will not get back all the cattle when his wife leaves him. The father and brothers retain always the rights of guardianship, and may remove the wife if they think it necessary to do so, the number of cattle, if any, to be returned being decided in open discussion. But if the marriage takes place, as it often does, before the whole of the goods have been handed over, the first daughter goes to the maternal grandfather or his heirs, and if she reaches marriageable age before the full amount has been paid, the cattle for her marriage belong, not to her father, but to her maternal grandfather.

Even apart from the question of payment, a native marriage is a complicated business, involving prolonged negotiations ; inquiries into the character and health of the parties, the prospects of the young man, the proposed place of residence, the quality of the gardens, and many other considerations, which are seriously gone into.

The first formal approach to the girl is made by a friend of the boy ; but as this is bad form, it is afterwards denied. Next, a neighbour of the girl's father is visited.

" My friend here," says the *mfusya* (go-between), " needs some one to carry water for him."

" There is no one here to carry water for him," says the neighbour.

" O yes, there is," comes the reply ; " the daughter of so-and-so would do very well."

The father of the girl is now visited by the whole party, and gives a non-committal consent, receiving a hoe as a token that negotiations have begun. Next day a council of the whole family discusses the proposal, and decides the number of cattle to be paid if everything else is satisfactory, with the pleasant prospect of a feast in the evening. The bridegroom and his friends then bring the first of the cattle, usually only one at this stage. The young men are oiled, painted, or adorned with leaves and flowers, and approach the bride's home at a run, leaping and shouting, and waving spears or clubs. The go-between lays on the ground a spear and a hoe, and invites the girl to come and take them. If she does so she signifies her consent to the marriage, but it should be noted that she has the right of refusal, though it is seldom exercised. Two brides recently refused in church (they were both Christians) to marry the men who stood beside them ; and a young girl a few months ago was with difficulty rescued from a hateful marriage, and is now pluckily living her own life, rather than submit to the unsavoury fate which her guardians had ordained for her. In case of refusal, however, the father may wash his hands of the whole matter, and decline to take any steps to find another husband for his disobedient daughter.

To return, the girl takes the hoe, and with the haft smites the cow which is standing there, in token that she accepts the obligations which the payment of the cattle involves. Then she lifts the spear, and hands it to her father, saying, " Slay me with this spear if I am unfaithful to my husband " ; and the father, with a grim assurance that he will not fail, lays up the spear in the house, where it will be seen by the ancestral spirits.

About a week after the feast which follows, the bride, with one girl friend, and a " mother," but not the mother who bore her, goes to the house of the go-between, who gives the mother a fowl, and the bride a piece of bark-cloth, and leads them to the husband's house. With a gift from the husband, the mother now retires, and a succession of small gifts induces the bride to take up her duties : a fowl persuades her to enter the house ; some other gift, probably a few cents, induces her to kindle a fire, a third to cook food, and a final gift is required to make her lie down on the mat along with her girl friend, who stays with her for a few days. This ceremony of the gifts is never omitted in heathen marriages, and each successively binds the girl to her husband.

If the bride is a twin, the doctor must be present, to sprinkle medicines over house and bedding, and to give the couple a decoction supposed to prevent the occurrence of twins in the new family.

Except the daughters of Christian parents, all Konde girls are married before they arrive at puberty, and what has been described above applies to child wives, who stay with their husbands for about a month, and then go home.

The child wife having grown to womanhood, however, further ceremonies have to be observed. The husband arrives at her father's house with an ox for the feast, and a mock struggle for possession of the bride takes place. The women of her family barricade themselves in the house, which is attacked by the women of the other family. Payment of a shilling opens the door, and the further struggle which takes place in the house is brought to an end by the formal presentation of the ox. The husband and his friends enter, and engage in a weird dance, a mere tramping of the floor in unison, with shouting and waving of spears, no doubt a survival of what was once marriage by capture.

The washing and shaving of the bride follows, and her bark-cloth is burned, and a new one given her, and then comes the feast of beef and beer, the materials for the latter having been previously collected from house to house, with a snatch of song at each door. After the feast the bride goes in procession to her husband's house, accompanied by a number of girl friends. The happy couple are chased along the road, beaten with sticks as they go, and advised to treat each other as becomes husband and wife. At the door of her future home a final ceremony has to be performed : the wife of the go-between pours water over the husband's hands, and the bride, kneeling at his feet, receives the water as it falls, and washes her own hands therewith.

There are strict rules regarding selection. A man may not take a wife from the family either of his father or of his mother, using the word " family " in the native sense, implying the whole circle of relatives from which each originally came. But there are countless bye-laws. A man has two wives from different families ; the son of one wife may take a wife from the family of the other, the two families not being related ; but a man may not marry the daughter of his paternal uncle, for the latter is his " father," and the girl is his " sister." The daughter of his maternal uncle, again, is his cousin, and he may not marry her, though there is nothing to hinder his father marrying her. The chief Koloso married his father's sister, to the great scandal of his people, although the " father " was really a very distant relative, according to European ideas.

The marriage tie is sacred and binding ; how binding on the wife may be judged from the laying up of the spear which is to slay her if she disregards it. The injured husband, too, has the right to inflict death upon the paramour. This is no mere tale of the past, but a grim fact of to-day. Just a very short time ago, two of my workmen asked a day's leave of absence to go and bury a relative who had suffered the extreme penalty at the hands of an outraged husband. Cases of this nature are very numerous, and are necessarily treated by British law as murder ; but native law still looks upon them as a just reprisal by the husband.

Divorce is granted only for approved reasons. The husband, when he believes he has ground for divorce, requests his go-between to take up the case ; but the latter will do so only if he is satisfied that the evidence is sufficient to secure a verdict in his client's favour. The woman's father fixes a day for the public hearing of the case, himself as judge, for there is an appeal to the chief only if either party is dissatisfied with the decision arrived at. The finding of the court is in all cases reported to the chief.

The commonest cause is unfaithfulness of the wife, which being proved or admitted, there is no further discussion, although the trouble is sometimes patched up by the gift of a cow to the husband. If a wife has conceived, and does not tell her husband, it is a very grave matter indeed, for she is assumed to be trying to hide from him what is not his, and an action for divorce may follow. Barrenness, if known to be of the wife, is a cause of divorce ; but not seldom the wife retorts the charge upon her husband, and cases are not unknown where, by mutual agreement, both parties brought the dispute to the test of intercourse with others. Again, if daughters die one after another, their death is assumed to be due to the disease called *kitasya* in the mother, and she is divorced. A wife who goes out in the morning while her husband is still abed, is doing a very foolish thing, for there is at least the possibility that she is providing ground for divorce. General laziness and uselessness, inability or refusal to carry out the ordinary household duties, if persisted in, lead to divorce.

On the other hand, while ordinary unfaithfulness in the husband gives the wife no ground for an appeal for divorce, no woman will tolerate incest by her husband, but will demand instant release. Beating a wife and starving her will bring down father or brothers in wrath to demand the release of their ward; but beating alone only if merciless and persistent. The right of a husband to beat his wife within reason is not questioned. There are other grounds on which the wife may claim divorce, and also the husband, but in both cases they are such as cannot appear in print.

When a husband's demand for divorce has been granted, all the cattle given to the woman's father are returned, along with the increase which has taken place. British justice, with more fairness, deducts one-fifth or one-quarter of the number of cattle (plus increase) for each child born, the remainder going back to the husband. The children belong to the father, to whom belong also children unborn or too young to leave the mother. When the time comes, he takes such children away, leaving a cow as payment to his late wife for bringing them up. The frantic appeals of the mother, when her child is being taken away from her, make a most distressing scene. I have been implored by mothers, kneeling at my feet, or rolling on the ground in agony, to intercede for them ; but native and British law here coincide, and, apart from an appeal to the husband to forego his rights, nothing can be done. And any interference is inadvisable for the child's own sake, for there is reason to suspect that fathers deprived of what they consider their rights, take measures quietly to put the children to death. In the past the acknowledged child of adultery was openly put to death ; to-day the husband may claim it if it is a girl, for a girl is " cattle " ; but a boy he, in most cases, entirely ignores.

There is formally no limit to the number of wives a man may have, except the limit of his ability to part with cattle. But while polygamy was always lawful, it was not always expedient : warriors were often monogamous in practice until they reached an age when but little fighting was likely to be expected of them. And there were always men who never had more than one wife, two being a very common number for others. While there is a sentiment among some women in favour of monogamy, it is a very slow growth. There are women who will not marry Christians, because the wife of a Christian, being alone, has to do all the work, whereas in the other case, many wives make light work for each.

There are a few heathen women who do not wish their husbands to take other wives, but many who urge them to do so. Another wife is like a servant in the house, and the position of the principal wife (who is not necessarily the first) is improved when her husband adds to the number of her more or less obedient juniors. Formally they are her sisters; in reality they are her servants, and must always answer her demands with the polite response " *ta*." The husband also gains in importance as he acquires one wife after another. When the children are grown up, they are dispersed to various villages, and the father is always " feared " in such places, because he has sons or daughters who will see to it that he is properly honoured when he pays them a visit.

Husband and wife take new names at marriage; but they are for private use only, the old names being used by their friends. The new names, which are given in the presence of witnesses, indicate that the old life is past, and that new duties and privileges now bind the couple to each other.

The position of the wife is guarded in many ways. Her father and brothers are always ready to take up her quarrel, even to the extent of fighting her husband if need be. She owns property, but she retains it only so long as she is a wife : divorce separates her from husband and children, and also from all the household goods of which she is otherwise mistress. The husband hoes the garden, but the produce belongs to the wife ; he may not take anything without her consent, even to feed his friends. If one wife

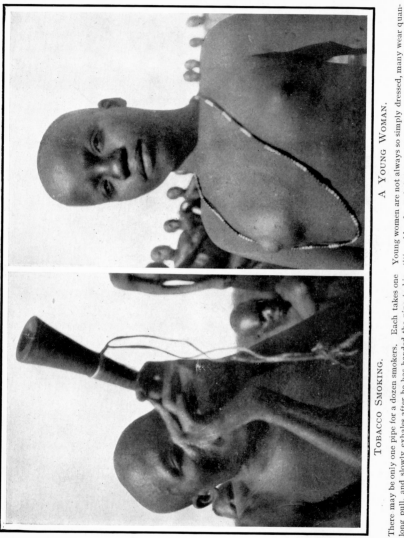

TOBACCO SMOKING.

There may be only one pipe for a dozen smokers. Each takes one long pull, and slowly exhales after he has handed the pipe to his neighbour. Many grow their own tobacco, and often take it in the form of snuff.

A YOUNG WOMAN.

Young women are not always so simply dressed, many wear quantities of beads on their neck and arms, and some are weighted down on neck, arms and ankles with coils of copper wire. The clean shaven head, however, is common to all girls who wish to be smart.

refuses point blank to feed his visitors, he appeals to
another; but it will be obvious that continued
churlishness on the part of a wife would lead to
trouble. Bananas, rice, and malesi belong to the
husband; bananas, because he alone attends to them;
rice, because it came from the Europeans; and malesi,
because from this cereal beer is made, and the husband
is lord of the beer pot once the beer is brewed. Fowls
belong to the wife, but though the profits of sale are
hers, she usually lays them out in small household
necessities, such as salt. She often gets a cow from
her father, and her husband may make her a similar
gift; and he must not use the milk without her
consent, though if it is sold, the money is laid by to
pay the tax. All household utensils are hers, except
the small dish from which her husband eats; but she
leaves everything behind should she be divorced,
except the cow she received from her father.

If a wife dies while still capable of child-bearing,
her father must give another daughter to the widower;
or, if he has none, a cow, dressed with flowers, is sent
with an apology, and a promise that as soon as possible
the dowry cattle will be returned. If the father
hopes that another daughter may yet be born to him,
an arrangement may be come to by which she will go
to the widower. Widows become the " family " of
the heir. They wear anklets of cow-skin, and let
their hair grow, mixing it with clay. These signs of
mourning they wear for about a year. Girls wear
similar tokens of mourning if either parent is dead,
but not boys.

E

The dowry cattle are usually found by the father of the bridegroom ; if he does not own them himself, the boy's uncles come to his aid ; and in the event of divorce, they are re-distributed, with the increase, in the proportion in which each contributed. The father of the bride, who receives the cattle, as a rule divides them among his relatives, one going, in the case of the first daughter to be married, to the village headman.

It is usual to commiserate the sad lot of the African wife. I am not sure that much commiseration is called for. If the husband converts his duties of natural guardian into those of oppressor, he will answer to her father and brothers. As I have indicated, she owns property in a small measure ; she is mistress in her own house ; even her husband seldom interferes with her decisions, and no one else ever does. She has to work hard, it is true, working up till old age at tasks that would quickly kill a European woman. But she is not unhappy ; indeed one sees more happy faces among them than unhappy ; and she is blessed beyond imagination in comparison with the horrible conditions in which some women in our own country lived during the earlier part of the Industrial Revolution ; and large numbers of them are happy in their husbands and children. Although many girls are married before they know what is happening to them, and many are unhappily yoked, as revealed by the great numbers who run away later with young men of their own age ; yet there are countless happy families, where deep affection binds husband and wife by strong ties ; and where a possibility of parting faces them, as in the case of men wishing to join the Christian Church, and so having to put away all wives except the first, it brings with it in very many cases a pain, keen and poignant, such as one might imagine would be felt by Europeans in similar circumstances. I know not a few cases where a young husband and wife began their married life by serious quarrelling ; but after a while not only became reconciled, but discovered that something had happened to them not unlike falling in love with each other. And, while there are too many instances of the opposite, it is further true that at least in the presence of strangers, husband and wife treat each other with a mutual courtesy and dignity, which would form no inappropriate model for peoples of higher development.

CHAPTER V

The Chief & his Counsellors

THE Chungu of to-day is but a poor shadow of his great ancestors. European power has deprived him of many of his prerogatives, and stripped his person and his office of much that was picturesque, and might well have been preserved. But even in the heyday of their glory, the Chungus were but priest-kings, hampered in their divinity, hedged in their kingship by advisers, limitations, customs, which could not be set aside.

To-day Chungu is but one chief among many ; but in the past chiefs of all ranks in the Karonga district were subject to him ; acknowledging his superiority, but yet asserting for themselves a considerable amount of independence, even to the extent of making war. First are the chiefs proper, chiefs of the snake, so called because their insignia of office is a buffalo or zebra tail, in which is a powerful medicine made from the flesh of a fabulous flying serpent, and which is believed to give its possessor great influence and authority. Next in rank, and subordinate to chiefs, are the *amafumu*, men who possess a less powerful medicine ; and finally men of still less importance, who exercise a strictly local authority.

Chungu himself, however, was, and still is, " the man who speaks with God " ; and as such he is hedged with a real divinity, which the limitations to which he has to submit, and the independence of the once-subordinate chiefs, have not yet destroyed. He remains pre-eminently the man of prayer, who carries to the ancestral spirits the petitions of the community, and speaks to them with an authority which no other possesses.

Far excelling in power and authority even the greatest of the chiefs were, and, shorn of much of their glory are, the *amakambara*, the councillors of Chungu. These men are in many cases chiefs of high rank, but even when they are not so, their position endows them with great influence and authority. The principal duties of the councillors were to put the reigning Chungu to death when he became seriously ill, a duty which has necessarily lapsed under British rule; to select, with the help of divination, his successor; to instruct him in his duties, to advise him in all matters which demand decision; and to depose him if he is unsatisfactory.

The health of the priest-king and the welfare of the whole community were inseparably bound up together. A Chungu in health and vigour meant a land yielding its fruits, rain coming in its season, evil averted. But a weak and ailing Chungu meant disasters of many kinds. Smaller illnesses Chungu, very excusably, concealed from his councillors, hoping that his ancestors would hear the prayers which he offered secretly by night. But when serious illness overtook him, the councillors were called to a full meeting by those who were about the person of the chief. For Chungu must not die a natural death ; the land would be turned into water should such a calamity be allowed to happen. Having decided that the illness is really grave, the councillors, one by one, give their voice in the formula, " *Siku na mwaka,*" literally, day and year ; but actually meaning, " Does God die ? " In solemn procession these terrible persons enter the house, and, having turned out the chief's wives, lay him down on the floor. Two keep him in that posture, while a third stops his breath by holding his mouth and nostrils, a fourth meanwhile gently slapping him all over the body until the life has gone out of him.

No announcement of the death was made. One of the councillors lived in the royal dwelling, so that if any came to consult Chungu a response might be given, and as he was rarely seen by common men, it was easy to keep up the deception. The councillors with their own hands digged the grave, and on their shoulders, at midnight, carried the body, anointed with lion fat, and enswathed in cloth, to the place of burial. Six or eight slaves, who did not return, went with them. Four went down into the grave to receive the body of their dead master, two at the head and two at the feet, and, in sitting position, held him in their arms. The remaining slaves being placed on the top, the soil was filled in on living and dead.

After the lapse of about a month, a big iron drum, now lost, was beaten, and it conveyed only one message to the people. " *Kutebite ku Mphande,*" Mphande (the royal residence) has done its work ;

Chungu is dead. Then the chiefs and their men, fully armed, gathered to the mourning. Weeping there was none, for Chungu must not be wept for; and women were not present, for the mourning for Chungu is war; quarrels may break out among the men, and there may be many deaths before the mourning is over. The chiefs bring oxen for the feast, and gifts of ivory to be laid up in the house where Chungu goes to pray when he prays alone.

The councillors now address themselves to the task of selecting a successor. There are no candidates; for not only must Chungu himself be helped out of the world, but all his sons, born after his accession, are put to death at birth. Daughters are allowed to live, and sons born before their father attained to the chief dignity, are not under the ban. Here again British rule steps in, but British rule has not yet been able to sweep all fear of the past out of the minds of the people. From among the *Bakerenge*, a circle of families within which the new Chungu must be found, name after name is presented to the spirits by the diviner, and when the divining rod indicates that the right name has been presented, the formula is uttered, "*Abapasi bitike*," the underworld has spoken.

At a great feast, at which all men of royal blood must be present, Mulwa, one of the councillors, by hereditary right offers prayer to the spirits, as if the selection had not already been made:

" Ye chiefs, we pray you to show us our lord, who shall be our leader in all things. Let him be the man of your appointing, not of our desire; to whom all the land shall look ; who shall go to the holy place to pray for us, who shall guard the sacred objects of lordship. Let him be our food and our shield ; let his name be safety for all. I pray to you, chiefs of the past, ye who kill or save alive."

Mulwa, carrying in his hand the " rod of lordship," stands out and looks around on the assembled chiefs. Suddenly he throws the rod at the man selected. Immediately he is seized, with a shout of triumph, " He is our food and our shield." The wailing of his female relatives, who weep as for a dead man, is drowned in the shouting and drumming with which the new Chungu is brought to the sacred house, where he is anointed with lion fat, and seated on the lion skins with which the house is carpeted. In this house are kept all the objects of which he is guardian, the tails of eland, zebra, buffalo, elephant, containing the medicine made from the body of the great snake *inyifwira ;* skins and heads of lions ; ivory, cloth, and the rod of lordship.

After about three months of strict seclusion, during which his health is carefully noted, lest, being a weakling, he should be a menace to the land, the new ruler is brought to the dwelling which in the meantime has been built for him, and his reign is fairly begun.

The person of Chungu was regarded with extraordinary reverence. He was not approached by the common people, who were not allowed even to see the man who speaks with God. An immense enclosure surrounded his dwelling of many houses, where he lived with his wives and slaves, and, always present, some of his councillors. The arrival of visitors was announced by the young men who kept the gates; but only visitors of very high standing were actually admitted to the presence of the chief. If Chungu left the enclosure wearing his crown of black cloth with long streamers, the people hid themselves. When he went on a journey, the older people claimed the right of seeing him, and even saluting him as he passed; the younger were rigorously kept out of the way. When he crossed a river the men who carried him must not allow his feet to touch water, which he himself must never touch with his foot, for a flood would follow which would do much damage to the country.

To maintain his dignity, the chief received taxes in kind. His gardens were hoed, and his houses built, by the people. If an elephant was killed its tusks, and part of the flesh, were brought to him. Buffalo was royal game, and the whole carcase was his; his, too, were skins and tails of lion, leopard, and zebra; tusks of hippopotamus, horns of rhinoceros. Once in two years each chief brought him a young cow; and a portion of all spoils of war in prisoners, cattle, and other things, was his due.

Out of his abundance Chungu gave gifts to favourites or valued servants. He received and entertained distinguished visitors, though not all were admitted to his presence. They arrived with horns blowing and drums beating, the leader shouting,

" Ho, ho, ho, we go to him who kills and saves alive."
On arrival, such as had the honour of a personal
interview, received his blessing, " May God be
gracious to you " ; the visitor lying on his back and
clapping hands. At parting, perhaps a month later,
he was pressed to stay, but the parting benediction
was given : " God be with you. May lion and
leopard and hyena, snake and tree and personal
enemy, be still before you. May you find your
family in health." Then taking water, and squirting
it from his mouth, he prayed the spirits to care for
the departing guest.

The duties and powers of Chungu, as they were in
the past, and, in diminished glory and extent, still
are, may be briefly stated.

1. First and foremost, Chungu is the man who
speaks with God, and offers up the prayers of the
community in time of war, pestilence, drought, or
famine.

2. Dreams by the official dreamers were brought
to him by the councillors, and measures taken to
meet the approaching evil by offerings at the graves
of his ancestors, and by personal intercession.

3. After consulting his ancestors, he decided questions of peace or war.

4. Along with his councillors he heard important
lawsuits, and appeals against the decisions of other
chiefs.

5. He confirmed in their position subordinate
chiefs when recommended by his council to do so.

6. The whole land being his, he gave possessions to

new-comers, and drove out undesirables ; but always with the concurrence of the council.

7. He gave periodical feasts to all chiefs and their followers.

8. In general, it was the duty of Chungu to keep the land in peace ; but no decision of his was valid without the approval of his council.

In the north, across the Songwe, the failure to attain unity of control had as its natural consequence the failure to attain the same imposing ceremonial as at Karonga. The chiefs each retained his independence, and what has now to be said applies equally to the independent chiefs of the north, and to those of the south who were at one time under the dominion of Chungu.

A convenient starting-point is the installation of the heir and successor of a chief. The installation of Reuben, which began on 18th September, and ended on 19th November, 1921, is typical of all, and the description which follows was given to me by himself.

On the appointed day he left his home, and accompanied by eight young men who were to be his subordinate chiefs, and official dreamers, and all the young men of his father's principal village, he went to the place which was to be the site of his own village. There good huts were built for him and the eight young chiefs, and mere shelters for the others. The first item in a long ceremonial was the tree-planting. The medicine man took two pots into which he put two *imbigita* (lion-making medicines), and having filled the pots with earth, he planted a young seedling in each, *indola* in one, and *imbandapanda* in the other. Pits to receive the pots were digged by the doctor, and held in position by the two most important of the subordinate chiefs, who, with closed eyes, filled in the soil all around. The two *imbigita* become later the two lions of the young chief. Every chief has these mysterious lions, which are quite harmless except to evil-doers ; if any common person creates or controls a lion, it is the duty of these two to slay it. No one may eat food at harvest time until a portion has been set aside for these lions. The two trees in time provide the shade under which the chief's court will sit, and as long as they stand his residence must not be removed from their neighbourhood.

The doctor now took a broom, and swept the dust into the faces of Reuben and his subordinates, praying that the men under them would be in number as the dust of the earth. All the old fires were extinguished, and new fire was made by the young chief and his fellows ; at present from two pieces of wood rubbed together, but in the past, the lower was the bone of a leopard or lion specially dried for the purpose. In the old warlike days this fire kindled the courage of the chiefs, but with the peace that has been brought in by the white men such courage is not called for. From the fire thus made, brands were given out to all householders in the district, and no ashes from old fires were allowed to remain in any house.

Next came the great medicine drinking, which was to give authority to the new chiefs. It is indeed a fearsome mixture : ground flesh of *inyifwira* (the flying serpent) ; heart and nose of hyena, which enables one to see danger ahead ; heart of hawk, giving power to see danger from behind ; and heart of the fish-eagle, which swoops down upon its prey. Thus furnished the young rulers can foresee the future, deal with the present, and be a terror to all evil-doers. This powerful medicine is drunk by all chiefs at their installation, and spread under the beds to make them see in dreams what is coming in the future. But never may the chief eat food that is not freshly cooked, for that would take away all virtue even from these potent drugs.

From that time until the 19th November, the young men led a happy, care-free life. Their food was daily provided ; cattle were set apart for them ; they did not shave all that time, and no girls were allowed to go near them. On the closing day of the ceremonial, the fathers of all the young rulers came and stood at a distance, and the younger brother of Reuben was given a spear with which he knocked on the closed door of the hut in which Reuben and his companions were waiting, and called out, " There is war outside ; come out." Immediately all rushed to where the elders were standing, and after greetings, the company formed itself into a boundary com-mission, to fix the limits of Reuben's authority. Finally, the same day, the new chief was married to the two girls whose offspring will be his successors. They must be daughters of men of note, not cowards in battle, of no reproach in the tribe ; and the girls

themselves must be free from any kind of blemish.
They drink a medicine weaker than that taken by
their husband, but sufficiently potent to make them
respected by all the other women of the district.

The death of a chief, like that of Chungu, is a
great event. An immense crowd of men and women
gather on these occasions. At the death of Mwafongo,
near Karonga, in 1913, fifty head of cattle were killed
for the feast. Of these perhaps thirty were the
property of the dead chief ; the rest were brought by
the mourners as a token of respect for the dead man ;
but for each animal so killed, an equivalent, an ox
for an ox, a cow for a cow, was given to the donor
from the dead man's herd, so that the herd left by
Mwafongo was reduced by fifty at his death. Intense
emotion is generated at these gatherings, frequently
leading to death. And in the past it was the rule
that a chief should not go to his fathers alone. If
therefore fighting broke out, and men were killed, it
was only right and fitting that this should be so. In
1897 there was a small rising against the Germans, in
which the chief Mwakalinga and many of his people
were killed. The chief having been killed, it was not
surprising that there should be a heavy death-roll
among his men. The death of Mwasulama in 1918
was followed, quite naturally, by the influenza which
carried off so many of his people.

About a month after the death of the chief, the
feasting is resumed, this time with immense quantities
of beer which has been prepared in the interval.
The new chief is now anointed with oil, and the

shout is raised, "He is our food and our shield." The successor may refuse to act as chief, in which case another is chosen by the *amafumu* (subordinate chiefs).

The duties and privileges of chiefs are similar to those of Chungu. They cannot be deprived of their position, but if a chief proves himself thoroughly unsatisfactory, his people may leave him, and come under another, who will willingly receive them. The position is not always an enviable one. A chief whose people leave him loses position among his fellow-chiefs. And he is not always sure of the respect of his people. In 1923 a decision given by a lake-shore chief so roused the wrath of some of his people that they cut down his bananas, a deadly form of insult, which in this case has not yet been avenged, because the actual perpetrators, though known to many, have not been disclosed. Under the British Government, the chief is responsible for the payment of the taxes by his people; he must see to the upkeep of the roads in his district, to the supply of carriers for the Government when asked to do so; and to the general good behaviour of his people. He gets three to four per cent of the taxes paid in his district.

CHAPTER VI

Law & Crime

LAW, morals, and religion are inseparably bound up together. The old idea, still hard to kill, that in the native mind morals and religion have no connection with each other, is the reverse of the truth; but African ideas of morality do not always coincide with European, and to this disparity may be traced the belief that there is no morality in African religion. The sinless man is the man who has broken no law. He is said to be *mweru*, without offence. Now as law and custom are one, and as the spirits are jealous for the retention of all customs that were in force while they were on earth, the man who is assured of a good reception in the underworld is he who has either broken no law of custom, or, having broken the law, has made the required atonement to the injured person.

Everything was settled in the long distant past by the fathers, and all one has to do is to conform. For the long domination of ancient custom in law, morals, and religion, meant that life had attained to a condition of stable equilibrium, before the coming of the white man set all in confusion again for many of the people. The ancient equilibrium was disturbed by

A Professional Dancer.

Note the wristlets and anklets, which make a jingling noise as he leaps about. He is stripped to the waist. His audience is in front of him. He has thrown his cow-hide shield into the air and will catch it as it falls.

Salt Factory at Lake Rukwa.

Large quantities of salt are manufactured every year under Government supervision. The heavily impregnated water is evaporated, and the remaining deposit purified, and separated into grades, before being offered for sale.

law-breaking, and the balance was restored when the law was vindicated. The idea that stable equilibrium means stagnation is alien to the Konde mind. To disturb the balance in order to advance to new conditions is a European, not a Bantu idea, and wherever the European stimulus has been removed, the wheels of custom drag heavily again.

A native court is not, to a white man, an imposing spectacle ; though no doubt it is fearsome enough to some trembling rascal, who has little reason to hope that his misdeeds will escape their due reward. The court meets under the village tree, or, if the weather is bad, on the verandah of the chief or judge. There the chief sits with his headmen if the case is an important one, and there are usually a few old men present also, in whose memories are stored up records of previous cases which may have some bearing on the one in hand. The persons concerned are among the audience, which sits facing the court ; and when called upon, they rise in turn, and conduct the case from where they stand. The native is a keen disputer. I have known a clever man fight his case with amazing skill and perseverance ; even after it was clear that the evidence against him was complete, he would go on adducing fact after fact with a dialectical skill that would not disgrace a European lawyer at cross-examination. If the judge is a man with a sense of humour, he often announces his decision by relating some well-known story, the point of which is taken by all, as, with expressions of approval or otherwise, they rise and go. Execution of sentence

F

does not delay, but is carried out immediately. The loser may, however, appeal to another judge for a re-hearing of the case. Compensation in some form, usually cattle, or hoes, or, in a few cases, a daughter, is the sentence.

Theft.—The extraordinary boldness and skill of the Nyakyusa thieves are widely known. Outside their own country their reputation is perhaps greater than they deserve, great though that is. At one place guards are doubled when it is known that Nyakyusa carriers have arrived. No European house has escaped their attentions, to the greater or smaller loss of the owner. They break through brick walls, enter by door or window, conduct their operations by day or night, with equal indifference and success ; and the speed with which recognizable goods are disposed of, adds to the mystery of their methods.

A white man was recently robbed while reading in bed with dogs beside him, the thieves quietly lifting and carrying off a heavy trunk, which they believed to contain a large amount of cash, before the owner knew that they were in the room. Another had the whole of his kit taken while he himself was in the next room ; a medical man had his hand-bag taken from his bedroom at about five in the afternoon ; in yet another case the sum of two hundred shillings was quietly carried off from a table while three Europeans were sitting in the next room at breakfast. Sheets have been taken off beds, and the owners knew nothing of their loss until bed-time revealed the fact. Rifles and accoutrements have been removed from beside sleeping native soldiers, and blankets taken from under sleeping men. A few months ago all the contents of a native house were taken off at midday ; and a workman of mine, returning to his home at five in the evening, found that everything had been taken in his absence, though his house is in a village of considerable size. Considerations of meanness never hinder a thief when an opportunity presents itself. One Saturday, some time ago, an old widow, in preparation for the Sunday service in the Mission Church, washed her one garment, and spread it out on a bush to dry. Having nothing else to wear, she lay down behind another bush ; and presently along came a man who snatched off the garment and ran, pursued by the shrill objurgations of the disconsolate widow, the only punishment he ever received.

The thieving community forms a kind of federation, and gangs are made up from many different districts. There is a family some distance from here which boasts that they were thieves before the white man came and taught them ! The thieves are known in the villages to which they belong, but they are never betrayed, either because of the fear which they undoubtedly inspire ; or, in some cases, because the chiefs get a share of the proceeds of the industry. The number of thieves, and the amount of thieving, has greatly increased since the British occupation of Tanganyika Territory, to the disgust of honest men, who openly express their admiration for other aspects of British rule, but are very frank in their criticism of what they call our softness in dealing with evil-doers.

The complaint is not seldom made that in this respect they were better off under the Germans, for the Germans had a vigorous way with rascals, while now criminals are cared for in comfortable prisons, while honest men suffer loss for which they get no compensation. Professional thieves openly jeer at the sentences imposed : good feeding, houses, fires, blankets, and back to your " work " in fatter and fitter condition than when you left it !

So openly, so far as their own immediate neighbourhoods are concerned, are thieving operations carried on, that both the doctor and the diviner (the two offices are often combined in one person) are consulted ; the former to find out whether the proposed plans will be successful, the latter to supply the necessary medicines. Watchers being stationed to give the alarm, medicine is thrown on the roof of the house to be robbed, to make sure that the inmates shall sleep soundly ; and on the door, to make it open of itself, as many seriously believe. On entering, the first man in begins by handing out all weapons, so rendering the owner defenceless should he awaken ; then a brand from the fire, which is always burning in every house, is waved about to fill the place with smoke ; and a third medicine is placed under the heads of the sleeping people of the house. If the thieves dig in, as they often do, the work is performed with remarkable silence. When the hole is big enough, a large banana leaf is thrust in and moved about, to test if the inmates are really sleeping. Then one man goes in feet first, for a spear-wound in the foot from a watchful householder is less serious than the thrust through the chest which ended the life of an incautious robber a year ago.

When everything has been handed out to confederates, the doors are opened, and the cattle taken out ; for the latter sleep in the same house as their owners ; a custom which is attributed to the conviction that in no other way is there any chance at all of defending their property. If the owner has been killed in the house, the cattle, I am assured, will refuse to move ; but they will pass over the dead body if placed in the doorway, and give no further trouble. Murder is a not infrequent accompaniment of cattle stealing. A woman was killed with a blow of an axe, not five miles from my house, because she awoke and cried out when thieves were making off with their booty. There is a story, which has been only partially confirmed by the police, that in 1923 six persons were killed by the owners of cattle with which they were making off. The cattle lowed while being removed, the owners were roused, and over-took the thieves, who were killed in the fight which ensued.

Old stories say that thieves possess medicine which make it impossible for them to be recognized should the victim waken up while they are still in the house. They ask him if he knows who they are ; and as death may be the penalty of an affirmative answer, it is easy to believe that it is rarely given. So confident are the thieves of the power of the drug, that they sometimes coolly arouse their victims, and compel them to cook for them. One brave man, thus occupied, suddenly thrust a blazing brand into the face of one of his spoilers, whereupon he and his confederates bolted.

The native law of reprisal is the same as the old American law of horse stealing—death on the spot if caught. The chief did not interfere in such cases. On the contrary, he was indignant if criminals of this kind were brought to him. He refused to look at them, and reminded the captors that it was their duty to kill them where they were caught : let them be taken off and dealt with according to the law without further parley. Hanging on a tree was the commonest mode of disposing of captured thieves.

But the Konde loves his cattle, and not all the fear of the thieves and their medicines will hinder some individuals from doing all in their power to recover their property. An old man came some time ago to ask the loan of forty shillings. He explained that he had been robbed, and that his plan was to go through the country offering to buy a cow, in the hope that the thieves, not recognizing him, would offer him his own animal. It is pleasing to relate that the old man's plan was completely successful. *Per contra*, thieves sometimes bring intelligence, of a kind, to bear upon their profession, and cases are known where they have actually charged the real owner with having stolen their cattle, and had them awarded to them.

In strong contrast to the Nyakyusa of the north, the people of Karonga, though they steal from each other, do not steal from Europeans. During five years residence there, I never locked my doors, and the only theft of which I had to complain was the pendulum of a clock taken from an open building !

Murder.—Murder is, from the native point of view, a much less serious crime than cattle stealing. But it should be remembered that British law calls crimes murder which are not so called by the Konde. A man who kills his wife's paramour has not committed murder : he has exacted a just revenge, and no more. In a case of real murder, the murderer or his friends usually pay a fine, or rather a compensation, of up to ten head of cattle ; and the loss to the family of the murdered man is further made good by the other family handing over a daughter. This girl must never be spoken of as a substitute, for that would cause her children, when she has them, to die. It is needless to add that under British law compensation of any kind to the family of the murdered person does not acquit the murderer. What follows, therefore, is purely native law, which, if administered at all, is administered only when there is reason to believe that the police will never come to hear of it.

When a murder was committed, the chief directed the friends of the murderer to bring him for trial, but if they chose to put him to death themselves, the case was ended. Should it be impossible to discover the murderer, a friend of his, it hardly mattered who, was put to death, and a wide-extending vendetta might be the result. When the law is satisfied, a formal reconciliation between the two families takes place. Under the guidance of the medicine man, who is master of ceremonies on all such occasions, a sheep, provided by the family of the murderer, is killed, and taken hold of by the parties, while the doctor divides the carcase into two parts, each side taking its share. Medicine is poured into a pot, and a red-hot spear is plunged into it. The carcase of the sheep, cooked with this medicine, is placed upon banana leaves, and the feast of reconciliation is partaken of, along with beer which also has been doctored. The reconciliation, however, is not complete until the girl has been handed over : until that is done, the feast has only stayed action on the part of the murdered man's relatives. If the murderer is not known, the relatives of the victim drink a medicine, without which, if they happened unwittingly to drink water in the culprit's house, they would themselves also die.

The murder of a pregnant woman is a very serious matter, for it is really a double murder, and the chief has to be compensated for the loss of dependents. It is more heinous to murder a woman than a man, for the woman, being dead, bears no more children, and loss to the community results.

For accidental death there are numerous regulations. If a man dies, or is killed, while in the employment of another, or on a journey with him, compensation must be paid to the relatives. There is no feast of reconciliation, for the thing was not done in malice. When a person is killed by an ox or a cow, the owner pays a cow, and kills the offending animal, lest it lead him into further trouble and expense of the same kind. If one is cutting down a tree, and some one is killed by its fall ; or if one sends another up a tree to get fruit, or for any other purpose, and the person falls down and is killed, a cow must be paid in compensation ; if he is only injured, some smaller payment is made. If I permit a suicide to take place in my house, I must pay a cow, for I ought to have taken better care of my house. If a man kills himself with my spear I come under a similar penalty, and for the same reason. If a woman suckles another woman's child and it dies, the law of compensation holds good, and a cow must be paid. Very many regulations of this kind, which it would be a weariness to repeat, exist among the Konde people.

The spear with which a murder has been committed is cut off short at the haft, and the blade bent over with a stone, and it is then hung up in the roof of the house of a relative of the murderer.

Murder is frequently committed by means of poison and by witchcraft; and in either case it is difficult to trace the criminal. As an instance : a man is very quarrelsome in his village, an intolerable nuisance in fact. After a while he goes off to work somewhere, and now is the opportunity to get rid of him. In a few months news comes that he has been killed in a quarrel ; but the quarrel was brought on by witchcraft. His fellow-villagers went to a sorcerer, and persuaded him to stir up the quarrelsome one to some disagreement in his new home, which would be sure to end in his death. No British magistrate would consider a charge of murder in such a case, except against the actual murderers, but the Konde will not be convinced that the real facts are otherwise than as I have stated. The clumsy methods of murder favoured by the cleverest of European criminals take an inferior place before the successful malignity of this kind of thing.

Witchcraft.—No crime is regarded with so much abhorrence among Bantu peoples as the crime of witchcraft. It is a crime against the whole community, anti-social, destructive ; and the punishment, in many cases, was death. That punishment cannot now be inflicted, but a recent Ordinance against pretended witchcraft has given much satisfaction to the people, even although the punishment is less than they think the crime demands. To them there is no pretence about it ; it is a grave reality. If the poison cup proved a person guilty, he was immediately attacked with any weapon that came handy, and as a rule he was dead before he reached the end of the gauntlet ; but if, as now and again happened, he got off alive, he lost no time in getting away to another district. In the not so very remote past, the guilty person was burned to death in his own house, and not always did his family escape a like fate. A special punishment was reserved for witchcraft by crocodile. This particular crime consists in bewitching a crocodile to kill an enemy. The criminal, when discovered, was put into the water in a large fish-trap, and left there until a crocodile came and made an end.

Adultery.—This offence is said to have increased greatly since the coming of the white man, who will not permit the death penalty to be inflicted. But the

Konde does not resign what he considers his natural right on that account, and will take his chance of the white man's justice, if he can first get in with his own. Dramatically enough, a case occurred while I was working at the first draft of this chapter. A man came into my office, sweating at every pore, excitement in his eyes, and his whole bearing indicating something very unusual.

" Well," I said, " who are you ? What is your name ? "

" I am Mwandobero of Mwakete," he said. " I have killed a man."

" So ! And what do you expect me to do about it ? "

" Tie me up, and send me to the police."

" It's not my business," I said, " to tie men up. Go to the police yourself."

" Can a man go to the police himself with a story like that ? "

" Well," I said, " I will give you a letter, which you can take to the superintendent."

" Thank you, Bwana."

A few questions brought out the facts, which were what I expected them to be. His wife had that morning gone off with another man. The husband pursued the runaway couple, overtook them somewhere in the bush, made a fierce pass at the man with his spear, and then ran the five miles between the scene of the crime and my house. A few hours later I met him, in charge of an armed policeman, going to discover what had actually taken place. He grinned a friendly greeting, and passed on, without constraint of any kind. It turned out that the man was only slightly wounded ; but most husbands in such circumstances "mak' siccar."

If the guilty paramour escapes, he goes to another chief, who receives and protects him, unless his co-sinner is the wife of a chief, in which case the man is sent back to meet whatever punishment awaits him. The woman, as I have already said, is liable to the extreme penalty also, but I know of no case in which it has been inflicted, and I think it is of very rare occurrence. An alternative punishment was to have her ears cut off. There is a woman living in the neighbourhood who, along with her paramour, suffered this penalty lately, but the chief by whose orders it was done was heavily fined by the administrative officer. Other punishments are still in use, which will not bear the light of print. A wife found guilty is divorced without further question, and the cattle returned to the husband. Divorce is often sought for very trivial reasons, but native courts will not seriously consider ill-supported claims.

Arson.—There is a general rule that accidental burning of another man's goods must be compensated for, by replacing all that is lost, whether that be a mere shilling's worth, or a house and all its contents. Arson proper, however, is a much more serious crime, and in the past involved the enslavement of the criminal and all his family. Not a few cases of arson are among the crimes that are common to-day. The church at Karonga was burned down in 1921, probably as an act of revenge against a Christian ; but a common

explanation among the heathen is that it was the work
of an ex-Christian who had died the previous day, and
took the earliest opportunity, in his new state, of being
revenged on those who had expelled him from the
Church. In any case the act cost the Christian community at Karonga a large sum of money. Burning a
house is a method frequently resorted to of " getting
one's own back " from one's enemy, and detection is
extremely difficult.

The Land Laws.—All the land belongs to the chief,
who divides it among his various headmen, and they
in turn give it out to their immediate followers. New-
comers are admitted and given lands by the headmen,
but the grant must be confirmed by the chief, without
whose consent no arrangement is final. This ownership by the chief is not mere theory, but, on the other
hand, the individual has practically permanent rights
in his property. He cannot be turned out at the mere
caprice of anyone, and he hands on his lands to his
heirs. Absence, even for many years, does not affect
ownership, provided that wife or friends cultivate the
land in the meantime.

The law of trespass was very severe in the past, and
would remain so if the natives had their way. Trespass, however, does not mean merely walking over
another man's ground; in that sense there is no
trespass. It means annexation with the hoe; and if,
in the fight which followed discovery, the trespasser
was killed, a charge of murder did not lie against the
owner; but if the owner was killed, the trespasser was
indicted for murder. If the case was remitted to the

chief, a cow was paid in compensation, for the man could not be put to death in cold blood.

A thief caught in a garden stealing growing crops is stripped of his *manyeta* (body rings) if he has them : otherwise whatever he has is taken. This law is still nominally in force, but the culprit often prefers to take his trial at the hands of the administrative officer. And the owner has no choice, for if he takes possession by force of what native law considers his rights, he is likely to find himself accused of an illegal act.

CHAPTER VII

Things Forbidden

WHEN the Konde wish to say that a certain
thing is prohibited, they call it *mwiko*, a
word which includes all that is more
popularly known as *tabu*, prohibitions connected with religion, good manners, medicines ; in
short there is a code of regulations which might well
be called the laws of life, were it not that they are in
all cases prohibitions, and never injunctions directing
one what to do. What is *mwiko* is what is forbidden,
and it is forbidden because it is disgraceful, wicked,
improper, inconvenient. No decent person ever
breaks these laws intentionally, but the punishment
for unwitting breach is the same as for the most
wicked intention ; it is in most cases automatic, falling
indifferently upon the well- and the ill-intentioned.
But while this is so, the punishment is by no means
inevitable ; medicines, ceremonies, payments, can
avert most of them, leaving little except the curse of
a father, and one or two other things, against which
there is no protection.

The native has no explanation of these prohibitions,
except that they were handed down from the fathers.
They are all the more valid for that ; buried deep in
the past, and coming upon each individual with all

the authority and mystery of the ages, he accepts them unquestioningly ; nor would his faith be at all weakened if he knew that in some cases punishment had failed to follow transgression. He would conclude that protection had in some acknowledged way been found, but he had not happened to hear of it. To break a *tabu* in order to see what would happen is an act of folly so extreme that only a few men can afford to risk it.

Anything like a complete account of the endless prohibitions which hedge the life of the Konde is not attempted here. He meets them when he first opens his eyes upon the world, and parts from them only when he goes to the land of spirits, where, no doubt, another set of laws awaits him. While he lives he has to be on the watch for prohibitions referring to God and the spirits ; to persons, acts, words, places, animals, and in some degree to time itself.

Thus it is *mwiko* to use the name of God unnecessarily in taking an oath ; nor may the name of the chief be used with too much freedom, *tata*, father, being his more common appellation. A wife may never speak of her father-in-law by name, nor a husband of his mother-in-law. Some parts of the body are *mwiko*, and are not named. Animals, again, especially dangerous animals, are more dangerous if their names are used, for the name calls the owner to the place where it is heard. A lion or leopard known to be prowling about at night is referred to as *tata*, father ; and if the animal is being hunted, one coming in later to join in the hunt must not ask, " Where is

A PUBLIC DANCE.

Usually dances take place at night, and many of them are morally evil, but daylight dancing is not uncommon, and is usually free from objectionable accompaniments. What is shown is a kind of solo dance, but commonly a circle is formed into which dancers advance, one or two at a time, to an accompaniment of drums, singing and hand clapping.

it ? " even although he avoids the name. If a woman about to go for water or firewood hears anyone use the word for lion, she will not go. An elephant in the garden is referred to, very strangely, as *ikisu*, the world ; a crocodile is *ikya mmisi*, the thing in the water ; and a snake is referred to as " the thing from the grass." The name of a dead person is not used by relatives.

Again, it is *mwiko* to see certain persons. Chungu, in the past, must not be seen by young people, though I have been unable to learn that anything very dreadful happened to them if they did. On the other hand, children are still kept away from great doctors, whose glance has power to kill them ; nor may anyone watch a doctor making up his medicines.

Growing crops and food being cooked must not be approached by unclean persons, for the uncleanness would pass over and affect the food or the crops ; as it would affect other persons if they came near the unclean. Uncleanness is transmissible, and the full ceremonial of the original uncleanness must be gone through by the one to whom it has been transmitted, lest it should desecrate the whole community with its living *tabu*.

Prohibited places are numerous, chief among them being graves, which are *mwiko* to all except the families to which they belong. It is forbidden to work when a dead person is being mourned for, but I cannot learn that a breach of this rule would imply anything except disrespect to the dead.

If we try to classify the prohibitions we shall find

G

that the classes tend to shade into each other, leaving
no clear line of demarcation between one class and
another ; but there are some that are quite definitely
religious, and with these we may begin.

It is forbidden to mock at the lame, the deaf, the
blind, the dumb, or persons otherwise unfortunate.
The wrath of God is aroused, and the offender will
suffer the disability he laughs at in others. " Who
mocks an orphan," says an old proverb ; " let him
beware ; God is watching him." To insult one's
father is a crime so great that nothing can avert the
curse which follows, and follows automatically. The
prohibition against the use of names, too, has in
some cases certainly, in others probably, a religious
sanction. It is *mwiko* for anyone but the family
representative to pray to the spirits ; though, in a
case known to me, where a Christian prayed in an
assembly of chiefs and others gathered for the purpose,
and the rain asked for duly came, the older people
acknowledged that the event justified the breach of
custom.

Omission of the customary funeral rites is disgraceful, and the dead man will not fail to avenge himself
upon the offender. A case came to my knowledge
quite recently where a son refused to perform the
usual ceremonies for his just-departed father, and the
life of his own son was barely saved, so every one
believed, by a timely surrender. It is an interesting
fact that no opprobrium attaches to a Christian who
omits these rites, nor does any visitation follow from
the spirit land, while upon a heathen the punishment

falls automatically. If the family "priest" becomes a Christian, and therefore ceases to pray to the spirits, no one will take up his religious duties until he has been publicly appointed by the family to do so.

To offer a blemished animal in sacrifice, to eat the blood of a sacrificed animal, to eat animals that do not divide the hoof, are all forbidden; though the double qualification, to divide the hoof and chew the cud, is not insisted upon. This has direct religious sanction, but whether the prohibition against eating beasts of prey is so founded, I do not know. The Bandali even now will eat lion's flesh, and at Karonga long ago, though not now, the crocodile was eaten.

Night belongs to the spirits, and certain things must not be done then. If a woman sweeps out the house at night, her husband will indignantly ask her why she is driving off his ancestors! The spirits cut their hair at night, therefore living men must not. If bark-cloth is beaten out at night, the cattle will die; and if food is pounded or firewood cut up, leopards will come, and kill cattle, and perhaps people. It is *mwiko* to clap the hands at night (except openly in the dance), for the spirits do so, and imitation might be regarded by them as mockery, not flattery. A fire should not be kindled at night, nor should one lie on his back if lightning is playing around, for the lightning gets at one more easily in that position. To sit in the doorway at night is to usurp the place of the spirits when ceremonies are being performed.

Animals in which the spirits dwell, frogs, lizards,

snakes, lions, crocodiles, must not be carelessly killed.
Kill a frog, and you will become a leper ; the spirit
that lived in the frog will see to that. Not that a
spirit dwells in every frog ; but why take unnecessary
risks ! As for the lizard, what harm has it ever done
to anyone ? The stronger and more dangerous
animals can take care of themselves ; but again, not
every one of these is inhabited by a spirit ; one that
kills people may be safely killed. The two-headed
snake, *Ndumirakosa*, may be the temporary dwelling
of God Himself, and must not be killed. The owl is
perhaps in a different category : it is a favourite
dwelling of sorcerers ; and some insist on killing it
for that very reason, while others say that to kill it is
mwiko.

Hair must not be swept up, but picked up, and all
foreign matter separated ; else death may follow,
either by witchcraft, or by the action of the spirits.
It must not be left lying about, lest goats should eat
it ; in which case the late owner will assuredly
become bald ! The hair on the chest again, must not
be cut, for one's children will die. All this no doubt
had a religious sanction in the past ; but no Konde
will admit that it is any more than a custom handed
down, and for that reason to be carefully observed.

The jealousy of the spirits demands that a child
dying during the life of its paternal grandfather, be
buried at the house of the latter, not at its own
father's ; that the child of a second wife be buried
at the house of the principal wife ; and that a man
who would die well, should die at the house of his

first wife, for it is there only that the spirits meet him ; and if he becomes ill anywhere else, he has himself removed as soon as possible to the place where it is proper for him to die, if die he must.

A man who has been falsely reported dead in a far land, must not, on his return home, enter the village without ceremony. Letters sent on ahead to assure his relatives that he is alive, are not enough ; his father comes out to meet him ; but he takes care not to see his son until assurance has been given that he is a true man, not a spirit ; whereupon the father throws some food over his son's head, and both enter the village in peace.

It is *mwiko* to kill a python unless one is sure that it is dangerous. If it is found in the feeding ground, and the cows that day give a specially good milking, then it has been herding the cattle, and is not to be sought for afterwards with hostile intent. But the boys who saw it must go to the doctor to get medicine. Further, God Himself may be in it, or the spirit of a dead chief, and therefore it must be watched for assurance of its friendliness. If it enters a house a fowl is thrown to it, with which, if it makes off, all is well.

Very interesting are some of the prohibitions connected with the white man ; and it is obvious that these are of recent growth, so that we actually see *tabus* in the making. It is *mwiko* to go into a white man's house, for the pictures on his walls are the spirits of his ancestors, who are specially dangerous at night, when they may launch an unseen spear at the unlucky wight who has had the temerity to enter so dangerous a place. Further, a man dying of that invisible spear-wound will almost certainly have his portion with the spirits of white men, than which there is no more undesirable fate. Did he not have enough of the white men here on earth? This fear of the white man is passing; but there are still old men and women who will not approach him, for they insist that he is God, and it is *mwiko* to see God. An old man died recently at Karonga, who had always refused to see a white man, lest the sight should smite him down. One of the teachers at the Mission at Ipyana told me that his own mother will not go near him when he has on a white garment, for that, she knows, is the sign that he is going to speak to God, and even a native is dangerous at such a time, for the power of God may break through to destruction. There is a curious belief still lingering among old people, that Europeans are forbidden to sleep in houses, but must come out at night, and sleep in pools, their native element being water; for they are water spirits in origin, a belief no doubt due to the widespread story that we came from the sea itself, rather than from some place beyond it. White people are supposed to hold it *mwiko* to weep for the dead; and indeed why should they, seeing their dead arise at once and appear on the walls?

Some great chiefs must not tell if they have been wounded in battle. These remarkable men have power to remove a wound from a fatal to a non-fatal spot, and so recover. When Mwakalinga, in a fight with the Germans, was struck in the forehead by a bullet, he immediately removed the wound to his leg, where it was harmless. His *amafumu* (subordinate chiefs), however, sternly ordered him to replace it ; for he had been toying with Christianity, to the disgust of his subordinates, who, seeing a chance to get rid of him, eagerly seized it, and Mwakalinga passed to his fathers. Mwafongo at Karonga has the same power, and there may be others.

War is attended with so many religious ceremonies that the *tabus* connected with it are best taken under this head. Cowardice in battle is *mwiko*, and the coward gets no share of the spoils. There is a beer feast as part of the preparation for war ; but drunkenness before a battle is strictly forbidden. At the approach of war, husbands and wives must not live together, and he who is guilty of illegal intercourse will be killed at the first spear throw, before he has had time to throw his own spear ; while a chief who is given to such acts will be defeated, and his men slain.

Prohibitions due to fear of infection are very numerous. One must not pass over the outstretched legs of another, for the offender will be " caught " by any disease from which the offended may be suffering ; but a slight nip in the leg of the other by the offender wards off evil consequences. It is *mwiko* to throw a spear at a hyena, for the animal may escape with a wound, and barrenness will result for the offender, unless he goes at once to get counteracting medicines. If your father comes to visit you, you must not give him your own mat to sit on ; he sits on a leaf, which is thrown away when he leaves you ; otherwise your wives will become thin, and will have no children. It is *mwiko* for an aunt to pat a nephew or niece on the buttocks, lest any disease she has may pass over to them. A man in an epileptic fit must not be roused ; he who rouses him will himself become epileptic !

The saliva is sacred, and is often used in religious ceremonies ; but to spit upon a man is *mwiko*, and may bring itch and scab if payment is not made. The kidneys of an animal may be eaten only if given to you by a chief, or handed on the point of a spear ; death of your children is the penalty of neglect of this precaution. Disease clings to the drug that is used to cure it ; what is left must be thrown away where no one passes, lest a chance passer-by touching it with his foot be smitten by the disease. For possibly similar reasons, the family of a murdered man must not have friendly relations with the family of the murderer until the necessary ceremonies have been attended to : the spear that killed their friend may kill them too ; that is to say, they may be smitten with a disease which reasonable men will trace to their folly in being friendly with hostile persons. The leaves upon which a man sat while his case was being tried have mysterious powers in them ; a sorcerer may make deadly medicine out of them : therefore it is *mwiko* not to throw them carefully away.

The blood of a lion killed in the hunt must not be

allowed to escape ; it has *ifingira,* the most powerful of all drugs, and is divided between the chief and the great doctors, who alone may cut up a lion's carcase. Another very powerful drug is *ilibobwe,* which, if cast into a doctor's house, destroys the virtue of all his medicines ; and if carried through a garden will wither up all crops ; it is therefore *mwiko* to possess it unless one is a doctor.

The code of manners includes prohibitions against speaking with the mouth full in the presence of elders ; the elders will curse the offender with dire results ; against spitting, for sorcerers only are great enough to dare, and one may be accused of sorcery. If a great man is passing, one must sit right down on the ground to salute him ; to sit on a chair or any kind of seat is grossly bad manners, and is *mwiko ;* it is followed by the unspoken but unfailing curse. Nakedness, even among the unclothed Konde, is a serious offence ; at the least a small apron of leaves must be worn, for sorcerers go naked at night, and a charge may lie against anyone found unclad. If a stranger, notwithstanding the prohibition against it, asks for food, it must not be refused : how do you know that he is not a friend of Kabeta, who will send lions to punish you for churlishness ! A woman must not eat while the males of her family are eating ; if she does, her husband will talk to her presently. When on a journey, the young men must go first to face the dangers of the road ; it is *mwiko* for the elders or chiefs to be in front. If two companies meet, they must not mix ; each keeps its own side of

the road, and all spears must be lowered from the
" ready " position, as must axes or other weapons.
It is *mwiko* to attend to one's personal comfort in a
public place.

The prohibitions connected with women are very
numerous, and only a selection is given. A pregnant
woman may not go near food in any condition,
growing, being threshed, or being cooked ; nor may
she go near beer that is being prepared. If she goes
out of the house, she must not turn back in the doorway ; the ancestors are there ; she must go right out,
and if she needs to go in again, she must do it from a
pace or so from the door. The penalty is the death of
the child she is carrying. An interesting prohibition
is that against going behind anyone, and it applies
specially though not exclusively to women. The
incised medicine of the person behind whom she
passes loses its virtue ; but the evil may be averted by
the person turning round to face her. A woman must
not sweep rubbish out of the house ; she must lift it
out ; to sweep it out is to scatter her husband's
wealth.

The younger wife must not begin sowing or planting until the elder has begun ; she must not sleep at
night nearer the fire than the elder ; she must carry
loads for the elder wife, and be generally in a subordinate position. There is no reluctance on the part
of the first wife to see her husband taking others ;
the more he has the greater is her position. A singular
prohibition is that which forbids a man to take his
widowed mother home to care for her ; he must care

for her where she is, or at any rate at a distance from his own house.

Twins are among the greatest of misfortunes; and along with twins are counted children born feet first. This subject is dealt with separately, and it needs only to be noted that parents are segregated, must not speak even to each other except in whispers, must not drink milk, lest the cow should dry up, or give only water. The mother must not pass behind anyone without asking for permission, which is given by clapping hands; nor may she pass her own father without a ceremony in which she throws dust over his head. This goes on until another child is born, or until about five years have elapsed.

It is *mwiko* for a dog to drink the milk of a cow that has recently calved; the cow will dry up. The same result will follow if strangers go into the house while cows are being milked. It is forbidden to common people to eat new season's food until chiefs and village headmen and twins have eaten first; and even they eat only when the first fruits have been mixed with medicine by the doctor. The first fish of the season must not be taken to the village. It is eaten at the river by the boys. It belongs to the spirits. To make a sucking noise with the lips is *mwiko*, being a token of impudence; it may also lead to accusation of witchcraft. Never steal from a blacksmith; the scraps of iron you steal will produce a noise in your throat like the noise of his bellows, and presently you will die.

For a man to see his daughter-in-law, no matter

how unwittingly, is one of the gravest of misfortunes.
"He will never die," say some ; but this apparently
startling fate means no more than he will fall into one
sickness after another, and finally will die in a weak
and undesirable old age. Others believe in a different
kind of ill-luck. The man will be accursed, and will
be unable to stand upright, but will be obliged to
crawl on his buttocks all his life, scourged by an evil
spirit which dwells in him. If the daughter-in-law
sees her husband's father, she has merely committed
a breach of good manners, and suffers no evil in
consequence.

CHAPTER VIII

Domestic Animals : Agriculture

AMONG the Konde the cow is queen. The people are reasonably musical, but no sound strikes more pleasantly upon their ears than the raucous bellowing of cow and calf as they return from the pasturelands in the early afternoon. No Irishman ever rejoiced in his pigs as the Konde do in their cattle. The young men sleep with them ; the children play with them. The cow pays the tax and finds the wife ; she compensates for injuries and wipes out insults. Feuds and bonds are based on and settled by cattle. They are the cause of three-quarters of the crimes, and three-quarters of the virtues of the people ; they are prolific in law-suits before the European magistrate and the native chief. Indeed, the song of the cow and the Konde might be extended to the dimensions of a small epic. The great majority of the men invest all their spare cash in cattle, convinced that they get at once greater security and higher interest than in any other invest-ment open to them. The total number possessed by the tribe is not less than one hundred thousand head.

Every animal in a herd answers to its own name,

and will follow the caller wherever he goes. They come to be milked morning and evening, and no cow moves until her name is called. The greatest insult that can be offered to a man is to sprinkle milk on the road behind him as he passes, suggesting, " You are too incompetent to provide yourself and your family with milk to drink ; I can spare some to mock you with." And each man is jealous of the quality of his herd. A year or two ago, a wedding party went to pay over a cow to the bride's father. It was not a high-class animal : a bystander threw a taunt, and in the fight which followed, two men were killed, and a number wounded.

The man is the owner of the cattle as a rule. It is rare for the wife to own any ; but sometimes a father will make his daughter a present of a cow, which becomes hers absolutely, to pass, with its increase, to her son at her death or his marriage. The husband also may set a cow apart for his wife, but it returns to him in case of divorce.

During the day the cattle are herded by the village boys, each family sending one or two in turn to the work. They have a thoroughly good time, though for the smaller boys it is rather a testing time of moral and muscle, for they have a severe apprentice-ship to serve. Cows are milked by the owner usually twice a day. No one ever salutes a man while so engaged ; if the milk stops, he will be accused of witchcraft. A visitor arriving at milking time will sit down and wait, neither he nor his host taking any notice of each other until the cow that is being milked is finished ; then the host will offer a greeting, but no further conversation takes place until all the milking is over. Even his wife will not talk to a man milking. And women themselves do not milk as a rule. I was once called to see an old woman who had been terribly mauled by an enraged cow, which she had attempted to milk during her husband's illness. What enraged the cow I do not know, but the Konde believe that it was the sex of the milker, though men also are sometimes injured by enraged animals, usually a cow suckling her first calf.

Milk that is not drunk fresh is put into large pots, and the milk of five to ten days added day by day. It is covered over very carefully, and eaten, when thick, along with potatoes, bananas, or other food. The whey, which is poured off when the pot is full, is also drunk for its cathartic properties. The pots, of which a family with a large herd may have up to ten, are thoroughly cleansed after use with boiling water, and then laid on the fire for perfect disinfection. Sometimes the milk is further hardened by being allowed to drip from a closely woven basket for several days, when it becomes hard and slightly tough, with a flavour like that of milk cheese.

I have more than once proved the sustaining qualities and pleasant taste of thick milk prepared in the Konde fashion. On one occasion I was separated from my carriers, and, about two in the afternoon, having tramped since six in the morning, I stumbled into a village, and dropped exhausted under a great spreading tree. The chief, observing my exhausted condi-

tion, brought me a grass mat to lie on, and then ran
to fetch a great dish of *amasulu*, as the thick milk is
called.   Only once have I eaten more welcome food ;
when, having been obliged to make a long detour, I
lost touch with my food boxes, and got two cobs of
soft, juicy maize from a garden I was passing through.
That, I think, was the most delicious meal I ever
made.

Polling of cattle is practised, but only for special
reasons ; if the animal is bad-tempered, or if the horns
grow into the face, or if it is desired to give the cow
a youthful appearance with a view to a good sale.
The polling is done by specialists, but the cow, carefully bound, is held by the owner himself.   Fine-
looking horns are scraped to preserve their appearance.
There is no gelding of bullocks, as the animals are
never used for work of any kind ; though European
planters and others have proved that they respond
well to training.

A people so keen on cattle rearing have naturally
developed some skill in the treatment of the various
ills that afflict their stocks.   Sympathetic magic plays
a considerable part in the treatment.   If a cow drops
one bull-calf after another, the doctor will give the
owner a medicine made into four great pills.   Then,
if his own wife did not have a daughter as her first-
born, the owner engages the services of a woman who
did.   This daughter she takes upon her back, and,
while the owner forcibly opens the mouth of the cow,
she drops the pills into it.   Taking another supply in
her hand, she passes it over the back of the cow from

A BANANA-LEAF UMBRELLA.

In April there is an average rainfall of 36 inches. Children go to school, men and women go about their duties, protected—more or less—from the downpour, by a leaf taken from the nearest banana stem.

neck to tail, saying, " You will now give a cow-calf."
What remains of the medicine is put into the stall,
and the next calf will be a female. A cow that kills
her calf in dropping it is given a medicine which will
prevent the recurrence of the fatality. Medicine is
also given if the milk is not satisfactory in quantity ;
and by rubbing in a medicine from tail to neck
specialists claim to be able to tell whether a calf in
the womb is male or female.

A disease which does not yield to treatment is the
work either of the spirits or of a sorcerer. Divination
is resorted to, and the particular spirit operating
having been discovered, the appropriate offerings are
made, and the disease will now yield to treatment.
If it is due to witchcraft, the chief is informed, and
he publicly announces that if the animal is not well
by next day, he will have the poison test applied to
discover the culprit. This, however, if done at all
to-day, is done in secrecy, for the chief who permits
the poison cup to be administered is liable to severe
penalties. But so universal is the belief in witchcraft
that the suppression of the poison cup is adduced as
the cause of a great increase in the number of sorcerers, and consequently of the general insecurity.

Cattle are sometimes deliberately poisoned. A man
has a case at court, and it goes against him, although
he is convinced that he is in the right. He is ordered
to pay a cow to his antagonist ; which he does, but he
first poisons it with a slow-working drug, and the
animal will die in a few days. The successful litigant,
although he knows perfectly the cause of the death,

H

rarely appeals, convinced, though without reason, that the magistrate will pooh-pooh his story.

In 1920 a lake-shore chief was fined a large number of cattle ; and the animals, removed to the hills where the veterinary officer lived, did not thrive. The reason is no doubt to be found in the different climate ; but the natives give two quite different ones : many of them were bewitched ; and others were given a slow-working poison by owners who resented the fine. But the fact that many natives willingly bought them when offered for sale seems to indicate not all held the two theories referred to.

When an epidemic carries off large numbers of cattle, the Konde assume a fatalistic attitude. There is nothing to be done : why worry ? In 1894 immense numbers of cattle died of rinderpest. After learning by divination that neither spirits nor sorcerers had anything to do with it, the people put it down to *Mwanjebe*, a troublesome godlet of the neighbouring Kamanga tribe, against whom there was no appeal, and no protection. They assume the same fatalistic attitude to the interference of the white man, and a supreme distrust of all kinds of injections has arisen in their minds, since the widespread injections of 1918, when many of their cattle died. The chiefs are credited with saying on that occasion, " If the white man wishes to inject, let him inject ! Why make him angry ? Let the cattle die rather." If this is true, it is a testimony to the immense personal prestige of the white man, but is hardly flattering to his veterinary skill. A warning was issued that the flesh of cattle killed by rinderpest should not be eaten, but the injunction was disregarded, with fatal results, and again the fatalistic attitude in the presence of the all-powerful white man revealed itself : " If we die, that is the white man's affair. They wish to kill us." It is useless to point to the recent increase of cattle in the district. The reply always is that the deterioration in quality, which began with the coming of the white man, and has continued ever since, more than balances the increase in numbers.

In comparison with cattle, other animals are of small importance. Sheep and goats are reared in small numbers, and belong to the man, very much as cattle do. Fowls belong to any member of the family, and each owns what he sells them for. There are many breeds of dogs, formerly used for hunting, but now mostly as watchdogs, in view of the prevalence of thieving. Dogs are as a rule treated with neglect, and pick up a living as best they can from the garbage around the doors. With a few exceptions they are cowardly brutes, possibly a natural result of their vile treatment. Occasionally one will come upon a man who has well-fed, well-cared-for dogs, and is very proud of their intelligence and courage, either in keeping off thieves or in tending cattle. The story of the two dogs which were shown the limits within which their master's cattle might feed, and kept them strictly within bounds, is not, perhaps, without parallel in other lands.

There is a very remarkable tradition that in the old days of war, and especially during the Angoni raids, a cow about to be delivered of a calf was rushed down to running water, and the calf, when delivered, immediately submerged. Then cow and owner ran for their lives, and when the scourge had passed over, the owner, if he survived, took the calf out of the water, resuscitated it, and let it go. The explanation given to me by a medical colleague of the conditions under which such a thing is possible, render it highly probable that if ever it occurred at all, it must have been very rarely, and even less in times of war than in times of peace. What is interesting, however, is the fact that the physiological possibility of it is known to the natives. I have not met anyone who has seen it done.

Agriculture.—St. Paul would almost certainly have told the Konde that they were " too religious " ; not because he would have seen tokens of their religiousness in the streets and villages ; no mere passer-by, and no indifferent foreigner, ever sees that. One must look deep, and live long among them, before that side of their life reveals itself to him with any fulness. There is hardly an act of theirs that is not accompanied by a ceremony of some kind, if that is religion, and to them it undoubtedly is. Agriculture is a highly religious occupation on that view, but hardly more so than many others. Leaving native Christians aside, the great majority of the people consult a diviner before beginning to hoe. He may say that all is well ; or he may discover that some spirit stands in the way of a good crop, and must be propitiated ; or that a certain piece of ground is bewitched, and no good will come of hoeing it until the spell has been removed.

If a spirit is to be propitiated, beer is poured out and petition made as follows :

> " Ye fathers, I am about to sow my seed. How can it grow if ye kill what I put into the ground ? If ye are gracious to me, let me see the harvest."

Finishing his oblations with the usual squirting of water from the mouth, he next day sows his seed in confidence. If there are no obstacles from the spirits he does not pray. Why should he ? There is nothing to pray about.

The ceremonies are practically the same all over the Konde country, but many chiefs have special practices of their own. A very picturesque ceremony is that of the chief Mwaisumo. When the early rains have fallen, and the ground has been hoed, chief and people go to the grave of the ancestral chiefs, carrying their shields of ox-hide. The chief and his headmen, standing in rows, raise their shields above their heads, and Mwaisumo, taking water into his mouth, squirts it upwards, and prays for a good harvest. Immediately all the people break out into rejoicing, dancing, shouting, blowing bamboo whistles, and drumming. The seed may now be sown.

The first hoeing is *ukusebera*, gathering the heaps of dry rubbish and burning them. But even this is not done without ceremony. Every man goes to the doctor to get medicine, which is put into the biggest heap in his garden ; then, when the wife of the village headman has set fire to one of the heaps, which must not be one of those in her husband's garden, all the other women take fire from the lighted heap, and kindle their own, first setting the torch to the large heap which contains the medicine, the virtue of which is carried to all the other heaps as they are set alight one by one.

There is a custom, now passing away, but still followed by a few, of throwing medicine into the ground as one hoes. Many use manure for fertilisation, but the medicines I am speaking of have no manure qualities. They are *unkota*, something possessing mysterious powers, the virtues of which are known by experience, but are not open to rational explanation. One of the best-known medicines of this kind is elephant manure, dried and set on fire, and the smoke allowed to spread over the garden. Where this is used it insures a bumper crop.

Not even yet, however, is all ready, for the seed must be doctored before being sown. A medium-sized basket is taken, and plastered on the inside with the drug, which, of course, has been obtained from the local doctor, who at this season does a roaring trade. Into the basket the seed is put, mixed with more medicine, and then sown. The object in this case is not, however, to secure a good crop, but to prevent the yield being interfered with. If even a sorcerer steals from that garden, he will sicken, and probably die ; or a disease will eat up his lips, and he will stand revealed to all men for what he is, a garden thief, and, it may be, a sorcerer as well.

Working parties are often formed for the hoeing, the group spending one day in each garden, and being fed by the owner in each case. When a headman's garden is being done, beer is provided, and the chief usually kills an ox when he has a party hoeing for him. The main crops are maize, cassava, millet, sweet potatoes, peas, beans, ground nuts, but many other food-stuffs are cultivated. Every village is hidden in groves of bananas, which need regular tending. Rice is grown for the market, and in the Kinga Mountains large quantities of wheat are cultivated. Every man owns his clump of bamboos ; many have a few kapok trees, some mangoes, one or two lemon trees ; and some European fruits are slowly spreading to native gardens. A few cultivate kitchen vegetables, but only for sale to the white man.

In a few places I have seen intelligently conceived irrigation, but never on a large scale, each man attending to his own needs in the matter.

Growing crops must be protected from numerous pests. Boys are stationed by day to drive off monkeys ; straying cattle eating the crops involve their owner in damages : elephants, no rare visitors in some districts, are driven off by drum and horn and wild shouting when they pay no attention to the small sticks which are placed in a corner of the garden to keep them away. Pigs are very fond of growing maize ; and where they are numerous, small huts, elevated on poles, are built in the gardens, and there the young men sleep and keep an open ear for the grunting which betrays the presence of the spoilers. Then one may hear the long shout of the watchers, who add to their shouting the rattling of dried gourds strung on cords stretched across the garden, and presently the pigs clear off, and there is silence again. Many kinds of game get part at least of their living out of human industry, and have to be laboriously guarded against.

For smaller pests additional aid must be sought. Field mice and rats, *indafu*, a small locust-like creature, grubs, wireworms, and moles, work great injury, and ordinary methods of dealing with them are vain. Take, at sunset, a brand from the fire, and walk over the garden with it, singing " *Kuki Kyaubili ?* " Where is the Unseen God ? and the pests will clear out.

The first maize cobs are taken to the chief ; then each head of a family presents a few cobs to his own ancestors ; twins also must be presented with early cobs, and it is only then that common people are safe if they begin to eat the new season's crops. When the chief makes an offering to his ancestors, it is usually laid at the *lupando*, the place where the village trees stand. The maize is eaten by mice, but it is credited to the " lion " which is the chief's guardian (Chap. V). In some districts a perhaps more primitive ceremony is observed. With a following of little children, the doctor goes to the grave of the chief's ancestors, and there roasts a few maize cobs, which he divides among the children ; on their return, intimation is made that all may now eat the new crops.

The food stocks in the barns are protected by a medicine, but this practice is falling out of use, though many still follow it. If a man is too poor to buy the medicine, he begs a handful of the protected grain from his better-off neighbour, confident that the protective powers of the drug are securely transferred to his own stock.

A man who does not hoe is held in supreme contempt, but he does not starve. His neighbours give him food, seizing the opportunity to add much sound advice. But lazy men are held in suspicion, for it is highly probable that they will become garden thieves.

When there is reason to anticipate a general scarcity of food, the spirits are invited to confirm or dissipate fears. The chief orders a collection of *malesi* (millet) to be made, each village headman bringing the contribution of his people in a small basket. One headman is selected whose wife makes the beer, the behaviour of which indicates the spirit's answer to the question put. The beer is poured into a large calabash, and thence into two cups, which are placed at the *masyeto* (graves of the dead chiefs). There they are left for the night, and if in the morning the beer is found to have risen in the cups, filling them to the top, the harvest will be good; otherwise it will be bad. If the signs are good, all care is cast away, beer is made in great quantities, and drinking and feasting take the place of the previous anxiety. But when the spirits foretell a bad harvest the utmost economy is practised, and the chief is bound to see that no one makes prodigal use of his resources.

CHAPTER IX

Eating & Drinking

WHEN the white man travels he has a number of men who carry his pots and pans, his plates and spoons, and all the paraphernalia of his travelling kitchen. His two dozen or so Konde carriers are well provided for if they have a couple of pots between them, or a piece of tin, usually a flattened-out food tin, on which to roast their maize as they squat chattering round the evening fire. What the white man wants with all that he gives them to carry, they do not know, and are not always interested. I was once seated in a remote village having breakfast, and a very simple breakfast at that; but I heard one of the villagers, numbers of whom were looking on from a distance, ask my boy, " How do you know what to give him next ? " What the boy replied I did not hear, but the interest in his operations was great.

The carriers take no food for themselves. It is their business to look after the white man ; it is his to look after them ; and I have always found that if he takes reasonable care to see that they are well fed and bestowed, they will not stint themselves in service to him. If nothing else is obtainable, they will be

content with maize roasted on a piece of tin, or a few
potatoes roasted in the fire. I have known them, too,
going perforce for a long time and quite uncom-
plainingly, without salt, or any kind of relish for their
food. For all these drawbacks are fully compensated
for when the white man kills game ; then they gorge ;
then the astonishing capacity of the native to take in
food is seen at its best, or worst. A friend of mine
once, far up in the mountains, killed an eland, and,
leaving his men to deal with the carcase, went to his
camp. His men kindled a fire at the ndkill, a sat down
to feast ; when they returned to camp in the early
hours of the morning, one man was missing, and his
dead body was found where he fell, killed by his own
immense greed, aided by a heavy rain which set in
during the night.

But while feeding arrangements " on safari " are
primitive in the extreme, the ordinary household
arrangements are by no means so. The housewife
operates with a great variety of pots, baskets, calabashes, and some women are celebrated cooks. A
possibly mythical story of olden times tells how two
chiefs went to war for the possession of a great
woman, who was the wife of one of them, and was
widely distinguished for wisdom and sagacity, and
for her unusual culinary skill. She was secured by
the attacking chief, and lived with him quite happily
as his chief wife ; an unusual honour, for it is a
rule that captured wives never attain to that distinc-
tion.

The Konde, like most Bantu peoples, are noisy

eaters. The loud smacking of many pairs of lips round the camp fire makes a quite surprising noise ; to which is added, especially if there is *nyama* (flesh), a sustained conversation carried on in a loud voice, making a din which is only ended by an angry shout from the European, who has himself long ago finished his repast, and cannot sleep in the uproar of the feast.

If their table manners in this respect leave much to be desired, in others they are beyond reproach. They carefully wash their hands before, and their mouths after eating. For the hand, the right hand, which is the " eating " hand, is almost their only implement ; but I have often watched my carriers make spoons of folded leaves, with which they neatly scooped up the cooked maize, or whatever else they were eating ; and I have myself frequently drunk water scooped from a passing stream with a similarly folded leaf.

The one great meal a day is a mighty feast, and one's girth is considerably increased when it is over. Little children literally protrude in front, and their entire nakedness makes the protrusion very obvious. But while the Konde look forward to the evening meal as the event of the day, the practice of eating twice, or even thrice, is growing ; and I have never known anyone being averse from eating, and that heartily, at any hour of the twenty-four. Eating by families is unknown, would indeed be bad manners, for the men eat first, and the women only after their lords are satisfied. A few Christian families are beginning to eat *en famille*, but the practice is not looked upon with favour. The open air meal in good weather of course gives way to the meal in the house when it rains.

The far-stretching banana groves in which the villages are hidden indicate one of the favourite foods of the people. There are many kinds of banana, from the tiny " Lady's Fingers " to the great plantains, half an arm long ; and they are eaten in almost as many ways. Some are eaten direct from hand to mouth, peeled and corded, for even the small cords which adhere to the fruit after the skin is removed, are meticulously attended to ; other kinds are cut up and cooked ; some are ground into flour, of which porridge is made, or it is added to the flesh pot to give flavour to the soup.

Maize is cooked in many ways : whole, mashed, or ground ; boiled or roasted ; mixed with other foods, or alone. The porridge made from maize flour is a greyish sticky-looking mess, wholly repulsive to a white man, and is often eaten without relish of any kind. Cassava, with the poison washed out by three days' soaking in running water, then dried and ground into flour ; beans, with the skins removed by parboiling, and pressed between finger and thumb ; peas cooked without preparation ; potatoes, often eaten with milk ; these are main food-stuffs, but very many small herbs are used, especially for seasoning, and some very pleasant dishes are often served up to feed sick and well alike.

Fish provide many a dainty dish. The bulk of the fish caught is half roasted over a slow fire for preservation; and in that condition it will keep for many weeks. A great dainty is the *unsusu* fish, which is roasted and ground to flour, and hung up in grass bags in the roof, to be used as required.

But the Konde is happiest of all when he has flesh to eat; perhaps because it is a rather uncommon event. His cattle are not primarily for killing; primarily they are wealth stored up and increasing year by year. But he kills when there is a birth or a marriage or a death; for all these are occasions when one must not think of expense; and a number of Christians now hold birthday feasts for their children in addition to the occasions I have named. Generally the meat is preferred " high "; and it is then cooked with banana flour, salt, animal fat, pepper, the latter an Arab introduction. A kind of pie is sometimes made, by cutting the meat into slices, and putting it in layers in a pot, the layers being separated by *mbwiga* leaves, a plant which has a curry-like flavour; and the bottom of the pot is covered with maize to prevent the pie being burned.

The Nyakyusa practise a method of preserving flesh which I have not heard of as in use elsewhere, though it may really be quite common. Besides the universal method of roasting the freshly killed meat over a slow fire, there is the running water method. The fresh meat is placed in a sandy patch of running water, and left for about three months; but it may be visited daily for supplies, provided it is again quickly covered up with both sand and flowing water. All this must be done at night lest the hiding-place be revealed to others, and the flesh stolen.

Bread is made of twice-ground maize with salt added. It is kneaded into loaves of about three inches thick, and placed in layers, interleaved with banana leaf, in a pot with maize in the bottom. This bread is often taken on a journey, and will keep for five or six days. Eggs are " scrambled," with milk and salt, in a broken pot, but this is a European introduction. No young girl will eat hard-boiled eggs; they produce a snake in the abdomen, which, of course, in turn produces barrenness.

Very unpleasant to our minds are some of the delicious foods the Konde rejoice in: flying ants eaten alive as they are picked up where they fall from their brief honeymoon in the air; crawling white ants, a horrible mass of moving life; the Kungu fly, found on Lake Nyasa, whence it comes ashore in dense clouds, settles on bush and tree, and is shaken off into small baskets, to be taken home and baked into cakes while it is still fresh. In Bundali it is said that some still eat lion's flesh, and once upon a time the crocodile was eaten at Karonga. Sorcerers are accused of devouring human flesh. A new grave is sprinkled with a powerful medicine which makes the corpse come up without disturbing the soil, and the ghoulish feast is enjoyed without leaving a trace of the deed behind.

To-day there are many, even among the heathen, who say grace before food ; only the older men now follow the ancient custom of laying aside a small portion of every meal for the spirits. But there are many superstitions nevertheless among young and old. There is a family at Itete which eats neither flesh nor fish, nor ground nuts, any of which cause violent vomiting. Others will eat fish but not flesh, and *vice versa*. Eland and bushbuck bring on leprosy in some families ; goat brings ringworm ; rhinoceros gives people a white skin ; and hippo is very dangerous in the neighbourhood of lepers ; for lepers are buried in ant-hills, but they soon remove and betake themselves to the water, and enter the body of a hippo ; so, if you eat hippo, you may be eating leper ! Nyakyusa women will not eat a fowl, for fowls in the night cry out the names of ancestors ! But a cock which gives a faint cry in the early morning is quite safe. There are many who have abandoned all these beliefs, but the vast majority of the people still cling to them.

Drinking.—Beer is drink for men and gods ; or if not for gods, it is a drink urgently demanded by the spirits. With few exceptions, it is offered at all religious ceremonies, but there is no special way of making the beer for the offering ; it differs from ordinary beer only in that the cereal (*malesi*) from which it is made is contributed by all the people, while that used at an ordinary feast is made from *malesi* provided by the entertainer. Even at these feasts, however, a little is spilled on the ground

SIFTING.

A turning motion of the basket brings the chaff and dust to the top, and a skilful throw casts it out, leaving the flour, which is now ready for cooking.

GRINDING.

As evening approaches, the rasping sound of stone on stone with the grist between, may be heard all over the village, as the housewives begin to prepare the evening meal. The flour falls into the basket in front, and more grain is taken from the one at the side.

by each drinker as an offering to his individual ancestors.

Great crops of millet (*malesi*) are grown every year for beer ; but if the other food-stuffs threaten to give out before the new crops are ready, the chief issues a prohibition against beer making, and the crop is used for ordinary food. Licences are now required for beer making and selling ; but this regulation can only be enforced in the neighbourhood of a magistrate, and drinking goes on without restriction throughout the district.

To make the full-bodied strong beer, *malesi* is put into a closely woven basket and placed in water for a night. In the morning, swollen to twice its previous size, it is put into a number of smaller baskets, and covered with banana leaf. In a few days it sprouts, and is taken out and spread in the sun, and when dry it is pounded into flour. Over the flour, again divided into a number of baskets, is poured boiling water, and the *unkese*, as it is now called, is left to cool ; it then stands for four or five days, when the final mixing with boiling water takes place. An expert comes to taste it when cool, and if he pronounces it good, the guests are called to the feast. The women, in long procession, carry the beer to the place of feasting, and sometimes drink along with the men, more often by themselves.

As the night goes on prodigious quantities are consumed, and the noise becomes terrific. Drumming, shouting, singing, tramping of feet are the accompaniments ; and at Karonga I have had to get out of

I

bed at midnight to break up drunken revels, and drive
to bed men who, though sternly refused permission to
finish the beer, vowed themselves, in drunken senti-
mentality, my eternal friends. But not always do beer
feasts end so happily. As in other lands, some men
become jocular in drink, others quarrelsome, and
many a Konde beer feast has ended in a spear fight.
Beer is an accompaniment of feasts given at births,
marriages, and deaths; but occasion of that sort need
not be waited for. The chief may give a feast at any
time; or a man who has been long away from home
celebrates his return; or the hoeing season provides
an excuse; but with or without occasion, an immense
amount of beer is drunk every year.

Light beer is made in many ways. A favourite is
made from sweet potatoes laid out to dry, pounded
into flour, and mixed with flour of maize, cassava, or
other material, cooked, and drunk when cool. Ground-
nuts shelled and ground, put into small baskets with
water, and allowed to drip dry, then mixed with
malesi flour, and cooked, is a common drink; as is
also a light drink made from the juice of sugar-cane
similarly mixed and cooked. All these are non-intoxi-
cating, and are taken along with food, or at any other
time as a refreshing drink.

Many of the more progressive chiefs are alive to the
injury done by heavy drinking, and do all in their
power to stop it; and native Christians who take any
part in a beer feast are excluded from the sacraments.
By the action of the Government in exercising control
over beer, of some of the better chiefs, and of the

Christian Church, a more enlightened public opinion is gradually being formed on the subject ; but it is necessarily a slow growth. There are a few chiefs who are opposed to drinking ; there are others who are almost continually in a state of intoxication, and their example does much to perpetuate a ruinous evil.

CHAPTER X

Hunting & Fishing

STRICT game laws have made hunting a thing of the past; or at best it is done secretly, when it is not a wild, excited scramble after some unfortunate animal that has wandered into the gardens in search of food. Before the white man took over the country, however, hunting was an important and regular part of the year's work. The diviner fixed upon a favourable day for setting out, and the whole community met for the preliminary ceremonies, when prayer was offered to the spirits, and through them to God. All quarrels must be made up before the hunters set out, and there must be no sin or strife in the village while they are absent, else they will not all come back alive. In hunting, as in every important act of his life, the Konde must be sure of the goodwill of the spirits, for a single angry spirit may spoil a whole season's work, and render abortive every effort of the hunter, just as he may bring to nothing every other kind of activity. This permanent possibility of interference from the underworld is one of the fundamental facts of the inner life of the people, and real understanding of the native mind does not begin until this elementary fact has been grasped.

Nothing was left to chance. The spirits having
been placated, the natural skill of the hunters must
be reinforced by medicines. Indeed it is not improbable that the native would say that the whole of his
skill and success is due to medicines and ceremonies.
The warrior goes out to battle armed and protected
by prayers, drugs, and a good conscience ; equally for
the hunter good morals, good medicines, are as important as reliable weapons and a steady nerve.
Unkota wa nyango, to ensure a good spear-throw, or a
straight aim with the ancient rifle which some hunters
carried, was rubbed into flesh cuts in the hands ; and
burungo, to make sure that the animal died quickly and
without a long chase, was incised into the arms ; but
more frequently, and more effectively for this purpose,
bulembe was attached to the spear. This latter is a
deadly poison, happily, perhaps, known only to a very
few, for a single scratch is said to be fatal. It is said
that the Germans tried unsuccessfully to secure the
secret of its manufacture. The poison is attached,
in a leaf, to the blade of the spear, and the thrust into
the flesh of the animal releases it, so that it enters
the blood, and causes a speedy death.

Women must not touch or go near hunting weapons,
which are kept in the roof of the house. The spears
must not be placed near the fire, lest the game, sniff-
ing in the breeze the smell of smoke, deduce the
presence of mankind, and make off. The hunters
must eat only freshly cooked food, for cold food
destroys, as it does also for chiefs, the virtue of their
medicines. Fatal results are sure to follow contact

with their wives before setting out ; and a wife who sins in her husband's absence, will cause his death on the hunting ground. The smell of clothes, like the smell of fire, would drive the game away, and there-fore leaves only are worn while actually on the chase. Hunters thus fully equipped are called *abarumba*, the rank and file being mere *abafwimi* (drivers). The hunt might last for four to eight weeks, and as the men did not return to their homes until it was over, huts were built in which they slept. The boy who did the cooking was not allowed to hunt, for his close contact with the fire would be fatal to success.

Thus protected, the hunters went fearlessly to their work. In ordinary hunting there is no danger to speak of, though wounded animals sometimes turn furiously upon their hunters. But who can tell what sudden dangers the bush will spring upon one ? I have passed within sound of the snoring of a gorged lion, and being unarmed, I could only pass on ; I have been charged by enraged elephant and buffalo, and only barely escaped ; and not once or twice lions have crossed the path not far from where I was. Such dangers the native hunters faced, armed only with spears or old breech-loading rifles, no doubt further strengthened by the consciousness of the numerous medicines by which they were protected. These, however, are incidental dangers : the actual hunting involved dangers knowingly and unflinchingly faced. I have myself been present when a native speared a wounded buffalo at a distance of a yard or two, dancing, waving his spear, and singing a song of triumph before finally thrusting his weapon into the massive body, and then pushing it over with his hands. It should be added, however, that more than one bullet from my rifle had previously brought the great brute very near his death. A keen man will go close up, as indeed he must, to an elephant, before spearing it.

Each tribe had its own hunting ground, and poaching was very keenly resented; sometimes, in the long past, even leading to tribal war. The feeding ground of the village cattle was practical sanctuary for game, as hunting among cattle was not allowed, lest it should lead to quarrels with the owners.

The commonest method of hunting was (and is) to dig pits into which the game was driven, and killed on the spears planted in the bottom. A great circle was formed, and the animals slowly driven into the area in which the pits awaited them, and those which did not fall into them were easily speared as they attempted to break through the ring of hunters. Traps baited with salt or other bait, are still in use. The trap is made of strong saplings, the uprights held in place by cross-beams, and bound together with bark rope. Over the entrance is suspended a heavy beam, the ropes supporting it being so arranged that the entrance of the animal releases the beam, and either closes the door or disables the animal. Open traps are set on game paths without bait of any kind. The animal pushes through the cords supporting a beam; the beam drops, and the victim may lie in agony for days, before the hunters return to see what has happened.

For very small game, an even more cruel form of trap is used, which may often be seen in the bush. A stout branch is bent down, and held in place by cords which are released at a touch, and the unfortunate animal is suspended by the neck, to struggle until death comes to its relief, or the hunter who set the trap returns to secure the reward of his skill. For elephant and other large game, a heavily weighted spear was so fixed, high up in a great tree, that the game passing under it released the fastenings, and the spear dropped between its shoulders. Great care was taken to set the spear exactly perpendicular; a little water was poured upon it, and the shaft moved until the drip from the point was in exact line. The hunters were watching at a safe distance, and immediately set out in pursuit of a wounded animal; occasionally, too, a man was stationed in the tree itself, to drop the spear with his hands as his quarry passed. Women must not go near such traps.

Hippo were often killed in pits, digged near the lake shore or river banks, into which they fell as they wandered about in search of food. A more exciting game was to hunt them in canoes with spears and harpoon. The harpoon was so made that when plunged straight down on the passing hippo, the shaft was released, and the toothed blade, with a rope attached, was firmly imbedded in the flesh. Then followed a scene which closely resembled whale hunting stories. The hippo rushes off, then turns on its hunters, only to be driven off with spears as it comes close up to the canoe, charge and repulse being

Game Traps for Small Animals.

The cords holding the door are so arranged, that the animal, on entering, closes itself in, and escape is impossible. Dangerous animals are trapped in strong timber enclosures, the bait a sheep, or a goat, or sometimes an ox.

Calico-Making.

Once widely practised by the Konde, but now almost obsolete. The native product is strong and durable. Dyeing in black and red is also practised.

repeated until finally the great brute succumbs, perhaps far out on the lake, whence it is towed ashore, to be received with the triumphant rejoicings of the waiting crowd, which has been watching the fight from the beginning. But if the hippo comes up right under the canoe, the chase is over, and the death wail takes the place of the expected rejoicings.

The bolder hunters lie in wait for the game, by water pools or game paths ; or follow the spoor over miles of bush. The leader is usually the most skilful man in the company. He knows the ways of all the animals, and the dangers that are likely to be met with ; it is his privilege, when the game has been overtaken, to throw the first spear ; it is his duty to be the last to run when danger threatens ; he must see to the safety of the others before he thinks of himself. Many years ago, in 1912 I think, I was following up a wounded buffalo, with two native trackers. When the brute charged, as it did three times, I urged them to get on ahead, but they refused. "No," they said, "you are wearing heavy boots ; our feet are light ; we will keep behind you."

A favourite method with some hunters is to lie in the water where the animals come to drink ; or if it is not deep enough, they dig a pit in which they lie, covered over with leaves and branches ; when the game comes to drink, it is speared by the unseen hunter.

All the flesh belonged to the hunters ; but a substantial share was given to the chief, who claimed all elephant tusks as his special property. The leading hunter received a cow, not as compensation for the tusks, but as a reward for his skill; the chief took the tusks without question; they were his *umwana* (child).

The flesh was roasted on the field, over a slow fire. Stakes were fixed in the ground, and a kind of trestle made, perhaps about two feet high, under which a great fire was kindled, and the flesh, cut into long strips, placed over it. In this condition it keeps good for months, but it requires prolonged cooking when it is to be eaten. This method of preserving the flesh is used to-day, when a European makes a good kill.

Dogs were employed for hunting pigs and smaller animals. The dog chased the game, which, after a little, turned and chased the dog, and was led to where the hunters were waiting with spears. Dogs were used also for tracking, and are said to follow all but the largest animals. There are large dogs of European breed, which chase leopards, usually in couples, but not always do both dogs return from the chase, and sometimes neither.

An unsuccessful hunting season was a matter for careful inquiry; for there must have been a cause, and it was the duty of the diviner to find it. Generally it was due to the never-failing trouble in the spirit-land, and when the diviner discovered the names of the individual spirits to whose meticulous ill-temper the hunting fiasco was to be attributed, arrangements were made for their propitiation. Beer was made, and each hunter took a small piece of the flesh of the animal he was specially expert in killing; and the whole company repaired again to the hunting ground, where they built a hut under a large tree. The leader cooked native porridge, which was eaten along with beer and honey, when the spirits had had their due. A small heap of the porridge was set down with a little honey poured over it, and a small piece of flesh was laid beside it. Each ancestor was named, as his portion was laid out, and prayer was offered :

" Ye fathers, we have brought this beer and food for you. Why are you angry ? Neither pig, nor bushbuck, nor any other animal falls into our traps. Give them to us, ye who give us all. In our gardens there is maize and millet and all things else. Why then do you hinder us now ? Why are our traps empty ? Be merciful to us. God be merciful to us, and go to the Basango " (a neighbouring tribe).

After this ceremony, the hunt is resumed with fresh courage and new hopes, and possibly a great success.

Lion and leopard hunting is not, of course, prohibited by the game laws, and they are hunted or trapped with frequent success. A short time ago a leopard skin was brought to me, evil-smelling, and ruined by the spear-holes which marked a fierce encounter ; and one of the hunters, showing me where the leopard had leaped upon him, begged for a little medicine to apply to his wounds. The idea that his adventure made him an interesting person was not in all his thoughts.

When a trap is used, it is made of very strong timber, and divided into two portions. In one the live bait is

put, usually a sheep or a goat ; the lion or leopard
enters at the other end, and in doing so releases a
beam which closes the entrance. The bait is quite
safe, if it does not die of fright, for it may be some
time before the villagers come with spears to kill the
caged carnivore. But more exciting methods are in
use. In 1922 a leopard killed a number of children
near Ipyana. Traps proving useless, the chief called
for a great hunt, from which his men must not return
without the body of the leopard. The brute was
tracked, and encircled by a great multitude of men,
armed with *isengo*, a kind of hooked axe, with which
they mowed down the grass as they slowly worked
towards the centre of the ring where the leopard lay.
With a great spring it escaped when they came near,
but was again surrounded. This time it sprang at
one of the hunters, seizing him by the arm, but in an
instant all the others were upon it, seized it by legs,
neck, body, wherever they could get a grip, and held
it tightly upon the ground while others beat it to
death with their clubs.

Lions are killed in the same unflinching manner.
In the same year, 1922, a lion killed many people
near the lake shore. A hunt was organized, and the
men, primed with much beer, followed the spoor.
Infuriated by two spear-wounds, the lion turned and
seized one of its pursuers, but a third spear-wound
drove it off. Again it was surrounded, and the order
was given not to retire. Once again a man was seized,
but the lion was surrounded by his companions, and
killed as the leopard was. It hardly needs to be said

that lives were lost in these dangerous adventures, but no compensation was given to the relatives, as the risk was taken by command of the chief for the good of all. A great feast was given by the chief on the return from the hunt with the carcase of the lion or leopard. If no one was killed, the rejoicing was great ; if there were casualties, the grief of a few was not allowed to damp the joy of the others, for a powerful public enemy had been disposed of, and it was an occasion for rejoicing.

Bird hunting is sport for boys, not for grown men. A knobkerry skilfully thrown at a sitting bird sometimes brings it down ; but bow and arrow, which are used almost exclusively for this sport, secure a heavier bag. Where bird life is plentiful, bird-lime is smeared on trees, and numbers are caught in this way. Loop traps, similar to those used for small animals, may be found anywhere in the bush, not seldom with a rotting victim still hanging in them. Drop traps, of a construction similar to that used by boys at home, are also used. A broken pot or a small basket is supported precariously by an upright ; bait is placed within, and the bird, hopping on to a small platform, upsets the balance, and finds itself a prisoner. In suitable places small lakes are formed, and covered over with a network of loop traps, in which numbers of duck are caught.

Two interesting methods are followed by the boys. In the evening, when the birds are returning to roost, half a dozen boys stand with branches over their heads, while others wave smoky torches, to avoid which the birds settle on the branches and are skilfully caught. The other method is to throw dust in the air, where birds are numerous, just after the young begin to leave the nests. The birds, " thinking it is rain," settle on the ground and are easily caught.

Fishing.—Fishing remains an important part of the year's work for those living near river or lake. For river fishing, huts are built in the vicinity of the place where the traps are to be set, for the fishers live there as long as the season lasts. Ceremonies similar to those observed before the hunters set out for the bush, must be performed. Sometime in May, when the river is in flood, the chief fisher of the Mbaka dreams of fish, a sign that the time has come to begin the year's work. A great quantity of *unkonda*, fish poison, is prepared, each fisher, and there may be as many as fifty, preparing his own. When all are ready, led by the chief fisher, they go to the water, and trample the poison leaves into the bottom of the river. The poison sickens the fish, which are then easily caught in the traps which are set for them with the mouth opening upstream. As soon as all the traps are set, the men lie down on their backs on the bank, and proceed to invoke the aid of sympathetic magic. They open and close their mouths, gasp, in imitation of dying fish. The probability of a good season is greatly enhanced by this process, which, though omitted now by many, is still widely followed.

The traps are laid in rows right across the river, and are in the form of immense baskets with gradually

narrowing mouths, so arranged that when a fish is
once in, it cannot get out again. Others are open
above, so that leaping fish fall into them, and cannot
escape. In the smaller rivers weirs or dams are
formed, and the water diverted, with much labour,
into another channel, in which the traps can more
easily be set; this is the case especially in streams
with stony bottoms. Fish spears are used, either for
thrusting at random in the water, when fish are
plentiful, or for stalking individual fishes. The spear
is formed with a long thin shaft, and small blades
with two or three spikes. When a fish is caught, it is
pulled off the whole length of the shaft, for the
spikes would tear the flesh if it were taken off at the
blade end.

Fish hooks are mostly pre-European, and barbless,
though some are now made with barbs. The bait is
fish, flesh, potatoes or bean mash, which many kinds
of fish are said to take readily. The line as a rule is
very long, perhaps as much as a hundred yards, and
is supported by small sticks placed upright at intervals
in the ground. Where crocodiles are numerous, the
bait is thrown far out into the water, and the fisher
retires to a place of safety, where he awaits the pull
which indicates a fish at his hook. If he would secure
it he must be smart, for the barbless hook will not
hold it long. This sport is indulged in mostly at
night, a fire being kindled to attract the fish; but as
crocodiles and serpents may also be attracted, it is
supposed to be somewhat dangerous, and to call for
constant watchfulness.

Women have dipping baskets without top or bottom, which they dip at random, and when fish is plentiful they get a good catch. Boys prepare bunches of worms fastened to a cord and thrown into the stream. Sitting down on the banks, they sing or whistle to attract the fish. A sharp pull when a nibble is felt lands the unwary fish.

Nets large and small are in use on the lake. The larger are furnished with stone sinkers and wood floats, and are operated very much as in Europe, a canoe feeding out the net, which is hauled in from both ends with the catch enclosed. The smaller nets are sometimes operated by one man, heavier ones requiring two ; and there are tiny dipping nets, of which a man will sometimes have one in each hand. Nets must be treated with medicine before being used. The Abakisi, a small tribe living at Matema near the north end of the lake, stalk the fish under water, and are said to catch all kinds in this way.

In many places the first fish caught is not sent to the village, but is cooked and given to little children to eat, the bones being thrown back into the water. The idea is that this is one way of giving the spirits their portion ; I have already pointed out that beer offered to the spirits is in some families poured into the hands of children, who drink it, though adults may not do so. And flesh offered at the family place of prayer (the *ikiyinja*) is similarly given next day to children, who are told that it is the gift of their grandfather.

The remainder of the catch is dried over a slow

fire, in the same way as the flesh is treated by the hunters, and is carried by hawkers over the uplands, where they get a good price for it. River and lake supply a great variety of edible fish. My list, which is not complete, has the names of thirty-two species.

CHAPTER XI

Arts & Crafts

AS I write there is a church being erected at Kyimbila to seat about seven hundred and fifty people. It has fifteen windows, each with three Gothic arches, and six doors each with its Gothic arch. This work was done, with only amateur supervision, by native workmen, of whom only one has had any kind of training, all the rest being young men, some of whom had never handled a trowel, and the best of them had not had more than a few months now and again at similar work. A good deal of pulling down and rebuilding had to be done, but the building, as it stands, with its buttresses and arched doors and windows, has a dignified and satisfying appearance. The carpentry is being done with the assistance of a trained man from Nyasaland, all the other carpenters being men with a training, or lack of it, similar to that of the bricklayers. The church is cruciform in shape, and the placing of the crown couples, if that is correct designation, was a triumph of ingenuity and patience.

Now there is nothing in Konde arts and crafts to lead one to think all this a natural development of what they did before. For the remarkable thing about these arts and crafts is their failure to develop at all. Hints and suggestions were there continually; yet nothing ever came of them. Iron was digged, smelted, and made into tools, yet no better tool for digging the ironstone itself was thought of than the hoe. Cloth was widely made on native looms before the advent of inferior trade goods, and needles, with eyes, for sewing mats; but the idea of sewn garments did not penetrate the native mind. Burned clay pipes were made to direct the wind from the skin bellows into the blacksmith's fire, but no one received from these pipes a hint of other possibilities. The idea of the wheel, with its boundless possibilities, did not suggest itself to the Konde mind, nor, so far as I know, to the Bantu mind anywhere, although hints of it were lying about, especially in the round tree trunks which were used as rollers when a canoe had to be dragged some distance from the forest to the water.

At every point the native mind seems to have been waiting for the stimulus which was to come with the white man, and which has led to an awakening, the full extent of which is not realized except by thoughtful persons. For already, after the comparatively brief tuitional period of fifty years, Central Africans are replacing Indians as Government clerks, as hospital assistants, as engineers on river steamers, as telegraphists; they do all kinds of printing and bookbinding, carpentry, and building; and they fill positions of trust which a generation ago no one thought they would ever be capable of filling. The Konde have not yet taken more than a small share in all this progress ; but they have made a beginning, and they will go on.

Among the purely native arts that of the blacksmith is held in highest esteem ; and the blacksmith himself is a man feared as well as honoured ; and joked about as much as he is feared. I think if there were a local " Punch " here, jokes about the blacksmith would take the place of jokes about the plumber which in times past found so frequent favour with the editors of the actual " Punch." He steals both your time and your materials. He tells you that your hoe will be ready on a given day ; you get your hoe days afterwards, and he has not used more than half the material you gave him ; the rest will go to make another hoe, which he will sell, perhaps to yourself. " As great a thief as a blacksmith," " as big a liar as a blacksmith," are gross insults, not to the blacksmith, but to the man who is compared with him. " The blacksmith gets rich out of other men's property," is another saying indicating the morals of the great artificer. Yet he is feared also, and such jokes are never made in his presence, for he is in touch with mysterious powers, and his ancestor blacksmiths have their own ways of conveying information to him. Quite recently a native friend of mine was talking to his chief, when a messenger came in hot haste to say that a hoe had broken in the blacksmith's hands. The blacksmith had gone at once to consult a diviner, and learned that the spirits were angry because no one was worshipping. " Go at once, therefore, and tell Mwaikuyu (the chief). Do you think heaven is

empty ? " Mwaikuyu said, " Why should we die ?
I will call the people to worship."

The most important products of the smithy are
hoes and spears. Of the latter there are about a
dozen different kinds, for war, hunting, fishing ; with
broad or narrow blades ; plain or with one, two, or
three prongs ; with long or short hafts. Axes are
made for cutting down trees, digging out canoes, and
all heavy work ; some are slightly bent, and are used
adze-wise ; a small one, very sharp, is used for smooth-
ing woodwork and finishing it off. There is also the
isengo, a kind of cross between a hooked axe and a
small scythe, used mostly for clearing bush land ;
and a long-bladed axe, carried by chiefs over the
shoulder, and serving only as an ornament.

Knives are made of many patterns and sizes, with
or without sheaths. A long spear-bladed knife is used
for grass cutting, and a neat small strip of iron, sharpened at one end, not along the blade, is used as a
razor. Arrows are not much used, as the Konde are
not given to the use of the bow except for killing
birds. Fish hooks were originally barbless, but some
are now made on the European pattern. Needles
are made for sewing mats ; smaller ones for sewing
breaks in calabashes, and others for sewing basket-
work. Cow bells, tiny bells worn by little children
on the ankles, anklets, and bracelets for women,
complete the list.

For lake-shore people, and those living near the
larger rivers, the most important wood-working art is
canoe making, and the average Konde canoe is a

fearsome thing. It is sometimes hollowed out, by burning and hewing, miles from the shore, even up in the hills, and has to be dragged down by long-stretching teams, who will be entertained to a beer feast when the canoe is launched. The tree selected is not necessarily a straight one. A bend does not seem to matter, and some amazing things are afloat on the lake, and in regular use. But the Konde are not sailors, and compared, for example, with the Atonga, half-way down the lake, the number of canoes is very small indeed. The Konde catch their fish by setting lines of traps across the rivers; only a few bolder spirits venture out on the lake with nets.

Many years ago I was travelling with a team of hill-men, and not knowing the men I had to deal with, I crossed a deep river, swarming with crocodiles, by the first canoe that offered, leaving the men to follow, as I had no doubt they would readily do. But I had miscalculated. Not a man would enter the canoe, nor had the jeers of the villagers any effect whatever upon them. Finally I called for the canoe to ferry me back, with the intention of driving my reluctant highlanders, willy nilly, into it; but the threat was sufficient, and four or five ventured, planting their feet in the bottom, and stooping down to hold on to the sides with their hands. Half-way over, the canoe capsized, the men struggled, blowing and shouting, to my side of the river, and one or two villagers plunged in to retrieve my bed which was floating gracefully down the stream. The rest of my carriers, notwithstanding the accident, accepted the inevitable, and were ferried safely across.

For the rest, the variety of woodwork includes carved walking-sticks, with straight, knobbed, or bent handles ; chairs, stools, pillows, musical instruments, and wooden platters. In the Bundali district remarkably good Rurkee chairs are made on the European pattern, with perfectly smoothed spars, and perfectly burned-out holes for fitting the parts together. The one in my possession might quite well have been made in a carpenter's shop, but the only tools used were an axe and a knife, and a piece of iron for boring the holes. Toothed hair ornaments and small wooden dolls represent the finer work ; and bamboo cups are decorated with pleasing patterns in poker work.

More important than the woodwork is the ancient craft of the potter. There is, of course, no potter's wheel, everything, from the immense pots, three feet high, down to the smallest eating dish, being formed by hand, built up, as regards the larger ones, by successive layers of clay, and finally hardened, after drying in the sun, by being put on a fire, while another fire is kindled inside. There is a great variety of pots, both in shape and in size. The very large ones are used for storing grain or flour ; and some Europeans employ them for storing water. A well-stocked house will have up to twenty pots, for water carrying, for cooking porridge, fish, beans, flesh ; and special ones are kept for beer making and drinking. The best clay is found at the north end of the lake, and from there one will sometimes meet with long strings of men and women, carrying ten to a dozen pots, hawking them round the upland villages, or offering them for sale at the local market at Tukuyu. The pots made at Matema are smeared on the outside with a dull red ochre, and the more artistic potters work patterns in red, with thin lines around the protruding middle, and herring-bone or crossed patterns from thence to lip and base.

I once slept in a native house in which there was a double row of pots, one on top of the other, along two walls. I was told that they were there for ornamental purposes, " just as you white men have pictures on your walls."

Basket work is done everywhere, and a great variety of baskets are made. Immense *ifituba*, for storing grain, up to four feet high, and perhaps ten feet in girth, are to be found in almost every family. Smaller baskets for carrying goods of all kinds ; wide shallow baskets for sifting grain ; others for serving food, and yet others for drinking beer. The latter are so closely woven that they will hold water, and are made from a fine grass, which is found only in certain regions. A new development of this industry is the making of articles to European, or native, order ; hats, table mats, baskets with hinged lids and divisions inside, almost anything can be made if a specimen is given to the maker as a sample from which he may copy what is wanted. Basket work includes also the large and small fish traps in use at the lake or on the rivers.

Net making is naturally confined to the lake shore

HOUSEBUILDING.

Among the Konde this is a leisurely process. Slim, one roomed huts often take six months to finish, and the workers go off for weeks to other duties. The men cut the trees and erect the walls, which the women plaster. The roofing grass is brought in by the women, but thatching is men's work.

and the river banks. Large nets, with wide or fine mesh, are made with floats and sinkers attached, pulled at both ends by means of ropes. *Ilitimbilo* is a net used only at night, when the water is beaten with flat sticks to drive the fish into it. There are also small hand nets, and special nets made for catching special kinds of fish.

Weaving is a very ancient craft, and may have begun with the weaving of mats, which are at present made from banana fibre, grass, reeds, palm leaf, and the tough outer skin of palms. These mats are used for sleeping on, laying out grain to dry in the sun, straining pounded maize, and a dozen other uses. Long grass or palm leaf mats are used by Europeans as carpets ; and there is a good trade in palm leaf bags for carrying rice, and great mats for packing cotton for the European market.

Very good cloth is still woven in the Igale district by the Safwa. The art was formerly universal among the Konde, but has now died out before inferior trade goods. At Igale the cloth is either plain white, or mixed black and white, though dyes for other colours are known. These cloths make excellent bath towels, and a trade could be developed if encouragement were given. Bark-cloth is very extensively made, and there has been a recent revival of this industry consequent on the exorbitant price of European goods since the war. Women wear the long *ilyabi* or loin cloth of bark, and nothing else ; but, especially in the Igale district, complete suits are now made for men, wonderfully cut and sewn shorts and jackets, and sometimes long coats. They look well for a few weeks, and then take on a dirty depressing appearance, and it is safe to say that with the reduction in price of Home goods bark-cloth will go out of favour.

Leather work has not developed to any great extent. Women use undressed skins for carrying babies; and men, in remote districts, use them as aprons. In Poloto skins are sewn together to form garments, and in the Kinga Mountains the skins worn by the women are pleasingly decorated with shells, while the leg skins are skilfully cut into strips and used as ties, by which to bind the skin on the back. They are seldom worn in front, and the Kinga women go in furs as to their backs, while a small bunch of grass alone clothes the front. Shields, wide and narrow; blacksmith's bellows of undressed goat skin; tobacco and snuff pouches, waist belts, caps, sandals; and long strips of hide for binding purposes, such as the haft of a spear, are all or nearly all the uses that are made of leather, if indeed the term leather should be used at all, as most of the articles named are made from unprepared skins.

Beads are strung into pleasing patterns by using various colours, and are worn in strings or broad bands, on neck, forehead, arms, ankles, shoulders. Children often go clad only in a tiny apron of bead-work, and girls in the Kinga Mountains wear similar aprons until marriage.

One European house in my neighbourhood is decorated with a frieze of crude representations of men on foot or on horseback, motor-cars, cycles, birds, animals, snakes, in astonishing variety, done in black or red on white ground by two native artists from Rungwe. Whether the ideas were supplied to them by the white man who owned the house, I cannot tell, but the execution is entirely native, and, although the total effect is weird rather than pleasing, it indicates possibilities which might be worth developing.

If housebuilding be included in arts and crafts, then the Konde people take a high place. There are at present some remarkably good houses at Karonga, of four, five, or six apartments, built on the European model, with properly made doors and windows; and there is, not far from Tukuyu, a house at present being built, with two storeys, T-shaped, the only materials used being the ordinary wood and clay. But the common Konde hut is a very high-class thing compared with the rude erections of tribes which have surpassed the Konde in other respects. Whether it be the older round type, or the newer square, there is a neatness and cleanliness in the Konde homestead that is sadly lacking in tribes that are wealthier, and more ambitious, but whose ambitions are only slowly reaching out towards improved dwellings.

CHAPTER XII

Amusements & Relaxations

I HAVE already said that the average African is a man with an abundance of spare time on his hands, and the situation suits him exactly. But even with him it may pall, and something more than mere lying in the sun must be found to fill the idle hours. A full account of the numerous games and amusements would fill a small volume, and a few examples must suffice.

Association football is now very popular in many parts of Africa, and Konde youths take up the game with zest; but it can be enjoyed only at Mission schools, or at Government stations, or wherever there is a white man sufficiently interested to provide a ball, and to give some instruction in the game. They kick from the ball of the great toe, as direct kicking with bare feet is impossible. To score a goal is " to give the egg " to the losers, a phrase taken from one of their own games, where a rubber ball is knocked about with sticks by two sides, to attain a given objective, when the losing side is said to get " the egg."

I was once present at a school concert to which audience and performers gathered from many different villages. The programme, when presented to me by the committee, contained no less than eighty-one items. I asked the committee to reduce it by at least a half, but after earnest wrestling with the problem, they returned and said that I must do the reduction myself. By the simple method of drawing my pencil through every second item, I reduced the programme to forty-one, but I did it to the mournful head-shakings of the committee. The performance was a mixture of native songs, games, dances, and Christian hymns, and dragged its weary length far into the afternoon. But there was compensation. Eight or ten boys of about ten years old came on to the platform, and gave a " show " of a European doctor examining people for signs of sleeping sickness, regarding which there was a great scare at the time. The little fellow who acted the doctor was nothing less than an imitative genius, the kick with which he finally dismissed the examinees being done " to the life," and it never failed to raise uproarious laughter in the great audience.

Of purely native games and amusements the number is legion.

Ingongwe is the large purple lump at the end of a growing bunch of bananas. It is rolled on the ground and pursued by yelling boys, armed with pointed sticks, each jabbing at it as it rolls, until one lifts it triumphantly on his stick.

Ikimbenengwa. Two pounding sticks are laid parallel to each other. One boy holds a third across, lifting and lowering it rhythmically, while another tries to hold it down by putting his foot on it. If he fails, the moving pounding stick comes down upon his foot, which is held between the two parallel ones.

Ikyula, the frog. Two sides at a small distance from each advance to meet, hopping like frogs, and, circling round each other, return to their places. Any who fail through exhaustion are the captives of the other side, and the game goes on until one side is captured, or all are tired out.

Eya kalenda. Children form a ring, with one in the middle. All bend forward, hands on knees, and move round in a shuffling manner in a circle. The one in the middle acts as leader ; if he turns to the right the others do the same ; if to the left they follow suit. The leader sings "*eya kalenda,*" and the others respond with "*nyama we.*" After a little the leader claps hands over his head, the others following and singing the while.

"*Turwe na Babemba*" : let us fight the Abemba. Two rows of boys kneel facing each other, hands on ground, heads down ; all sing "*Turwe na Babemba*" twice, beating the ground with their hands. At the second singing one side advances on hands and knees, growling, to drive back the enemy ; then the other side advances to fight the first, and so on.

Pamba nsilili is not unlike " See the robbers passing by " or " Oranges and Lemons." Two of the tallest children stand facing each other, hands raised and meeting to form an arch, a gentle clapping being kept up all the time. The others form in line according to height, and sing "*E ! yuba nsilili* " ; the two forming the arch respond with "*Pamba nsilili.*"

Then the line advances and passes under the arch
singing. The last to pass through is usually held,
but sometimes escapes.

Of such games there is almost no end, and new ones
are continually being invented, many of them imitative of something introduced by the white man,
European peculiarities being specially liable to this
hilarious form of flattery. I have seen boys imitate
the peculiar walk of Europeans, to the intense joy of
the onlookers. For, let it be repeated, to the younger
generation the white man is no longer a little tin god,
or any other kind of god. He is fully respected for
all that the native considers worthy of respect (and
their ideas do not always harmonize with ours), but
if he is laughable for any reason, he need not doubt
that he is laughed at.

Dancing is the principal relaxation of the Konde,
if the violent exercise which it sometimes involves
may be called relaxation. It is indulged in with great
zest, and, as the night advances, with complete
abandon, moral and physical. There is not much
that can be called religious dancing: a children's
rain dance, a pestilence dance, and the wild leaping
and shouting, with horn and drum, which young and
old engage in at times of eclipse or earthquake. But
anything may be made the occasion of an impromptu
dance : the arrival of a European, especially if he is
popular ; the killing of lion or leopard ; the killing of
much game by a European ; the return of friends
from a journey ; or a score of other reasons, some of
them trivial, such as the laying down of a load which

a man has been carrying until he is almost exhausted ; but he has always enough strength in hand to enable him to give a few leaps of joy when he is at last set free from its weight.

The ordinary dance usually takes place at night. The dancers are summoned by the sound of the drum, which is an invitation to all who care to join. The general characteristics of all dances are movements and posturings of the body, usually two or more dancers, sometimes only one, advancing to the centre, making a few posturings or leaps, and retiring to give place to others, while the drums sound continuously, and the shouts of the dancers increase in vigour as the movement reaches its climax, until the noise becomes terrific and indescribable. And yet the older people, long past the dancing age, sleep soundly through the din ; though occasionally an angry man will get up and drive away a few boys and girls who have got up an impromptu dance after their elders are in bed.

Ikimbimbi dance. Men and women stand in opposing lines, the men carrying spears, the women rods. Two or three drums are beating, and at a signal all break out into a song, while simultaneously the lines advance to meet each other, and then fall back. Two men and two women dance into the centre, retire, and give place to others, until all have danced. The dancing is a mere shuffling of the feet with posturings, but the men and women do not touch each other. The singing is a recitative, with shouts intervening, and the drums beat softly or furiously in harmony with the singing.

[*Major J. S. Wells.*]

MEN'S DANCE.

The men's dance is often a procession with horns and drums, and waving buffalo tails, moving slowly in a circle. An individual will stand out and indulge in a wild *pas seul*, while the others move round.

Ingwata. Two lines as before, men and women advancing and retiring, while all the others keep up a continuous tramping more or less in time with the drums.

Amasere. Each dancer has half a dozen reeds filled at the top with sand, which they beat on the ground, while the lines advance and retire, and a man and a woman approach the centre, dance round each other, and give place to the next couple, singing and shouting as before.

Ikindundulu. In this dance there are no drums, but the opposing lines keep up a continuous shouting or singing ; two men advance to the women's line, one of whom comes out to meet them, selects the more handsome, and retires with him to her own line, which dances round him, laughing the while at the other, and later dancing round him with mocking songs. Two more men face the ordeal, until all have been through it.

Ikinanda. No drums, but each dancer has tiny calabashes, filled with sand, on the ankles, and two streamers of bark rope flowing out behind. The line advance and retire, giving place to couples who dance in the centre, while the others shout and clap hands.

Ikisepe. Each dancer has pieces of cloth or bark rope, one before, the other behind, and a reed in the hand ; the dance consists of heaves of the body which cause the streamers to be thrown out before and behind, while the drums beat and the song goes on, as each couple fills the centre for a moment.

L

Ikikweta. This a highly objectionable dance, better not too minutely described. There are four drums and uproarious singing and shouting. The dance is of recent introduction among the Konde, and is held late at night. The chiefs try to put it down, but without much success; and there are other very evil dances, which no decent people will have anything to do with. Such dances usually come like an epidemic, spread rapidly over a whole district, and lead to great moral injury, until they are put down by vigorous chiefs, or die out of themselves, until the epidemic comes round again. Very frequently these evil performances go on the whole night, with terrific noise, and so determined are the dancers, that respectable people are afraid to interfere, lest an unmerciful handling should send them back to their homes bruised and bleeding. But the approach of a white man sends the dancers rushing off to hide in the bush, as I have often found at all hours of the night.

Of games of skill the most important is a kind of draughts game, an Arab introduction. Thirty-six holes are made in the ground; the players, two or four in number, have small stones which they move from hole to hole, until one side is declared winner. I do not understand the game, and shall not attempt to describe it; but a very complete description is given in "The Ila-speaking Peoples," by Smith and Dale.

A favourite intellectual exercise is the propounding of riddles, of which there is a large stock, and new ones are always being added.   The following are a few examples :

My house has no doors ?   An egg.

My hen lays her eggs among thorns ?   A pineapple.

When I returned from my walk, I took the cow by the tail ?   A long-handled drinking calabash.

By day or by night, by hill or by plain, it is hard work ?   Walking on slippery ground.

I hoed a large garden, but when I gathered the crop it did not fill my hand ?   Haircutting.

All my children have red hats ?   The finger-nails.

It has neither feet to walk with, nor hands to seize with, yet it devours everything ?   Fire.

The chief's cup is empty ?   In comparison with the lake, which is always full.

Feet which have no toe-nails ?   The feet of a table.

The " wisdom of the fathers " is expressed in short pithy parables, of which the following are a few examples :

A familiar road needs no sign-posts.

If one fish (in a basket) rots, they all rot.   (Beware of evil company.)

The tongue has no bones.   (Beware of talkative people.)

The liar has only a short way to go.   (Your sin will find you out.)

Righteousness injures no one.

Little by little, and the cup is filled.   (Much dropping wears away stones.)

A hired man eats his own share and that of others. (Be self-reliant.)

The right hand does not cut off the left. (Be consistent.)

There is no blessing in hurry. (Think before you leap.)

If you would get something from under the bed, you must kneel down. (Honour to whom honour is due.)

If you would get honey, you must use fire. (Take the bull by the horns.)

Tales told to the children, and to adults, are as numerous as proverbs and riddles, or even more so. Many of them have come down the generations, but others are of quite recent origin; those which contain references to Europeans being necessarily late compositions, though in a few cases they may be old stories revised to suit modern conditions. At the concert referred to at the beginning of this chapter, one of the items was a hugely comic account of a native's adventures among Europeans, which quite convulsed the audience, though the white man was not always represented as getting the worst of the situation. The reciter, however, modestly disclaimed authorship, and assured me that he had received it from others. In any case the ability to tell a vivid story, and to show the humorous side of life, was quite striking.

These stories cover every aspect of life, and each one has a moral, not always obvious to the European listener, but apparently quite clear to the people themselves. They form part of the education of every child, and of the admonitory stock-in-trade of all parents of growing boys and girls. A judge will use one to give point to his decision ; a man pleading his case at the native court will illustrate his plea with an apt story. There are men and women whose large stock of tales, and skill in relating them, make them welcome in every gathering ; but anyone, on occasion, will tell one.

The Tortoise and the Hedgehog

Once upon a time, when there was a famine, the Tortoise went to a far country to buy food. He found it in abundance, and made up a load ; but on his way home he came upon a tree which had fallen across the path. So he laid down his load on the path, and followed the tree to see how big it was. When he was satisfied, he returned to pick up his load, but found that the Hedgehog had carried it off. Then the Tortoise said, " My friend Hedgehog, why have you taken off my load ? " " Your load ! " said the Hedgehog. " Why did you leave your load on the path ? No, I have beaten you." The Tortoise went at once to the judge, who summoned the Hedgehog ; and when he heard the facts he gave judgment for the latter. The judge said to the Tortoise, " You have lost the case. Why did you leave your load on the path ? You are a fool." So the Tortoise went home, and the Hedgehog went off with the load of food.

After a long time hunters went out to hunt the

Hedgehog, who, to escape from them, backed into a hole in the ground. And in that hole who was there but the Tortoise, who when he saw the tail of the Hedgehog coming in, promptly bit it off close to the bone, and said, " Now I've got you ! " The Hedgehog was terribly angry, and went off to the judge. The judge summoned the Tortoise, who said, " Why did he separate himself from his tail in that way ? The rest of us are all of a piece." And the judge said, " You are a fool, Hedgehog. Why don't you go like other people ? You have lost the case."

CHAPTER XIII

Konde Warfare

THE men of Munsoso were hunting, and came to the land of Mwakarobo with their " bag." Mwakarobo's men crept up while the tired hunters were resting in the shade of the trees, and carried off the birds.

" Why do you steal our birds ? " demanded the angry hunters.

" We don't talk with fools," sneeringly replied the others, as they went off with the booty ; " get off home, or one man of us will chase the lot of you."

Home the hunters went, and great was the uproar in the village when the tale was told. " I am an old man," cried the indignant chief, " but we must fight."

" Don't speak of it," said his sons, " let the spear talk."

Next day the fighting men went forth at dawn, and burned a few huts in Mwakarobo's village, from which the defenders, unable to prepare a defence, had removed all the women and cattle. A few days later, having made an alliance with some neighbouring chiefs, Munsoso attacked in force, and drove Mwakarobo out of his country, which to this day he has never recovered.

Not all Konde wars arose from such trivial causes, or had results so trifling ; but much of it was of this petty nature : wife stealing, cattle stealing, insults, civil war to drive out an unpopular chief, were among the causes. More important were the wars waged to acquire new territory, as in the wars of the first Chungu, and the conquests made by the Sango and Kinga chiefs some generations ago. There were, properly speaking, no religious wars, nor was there any desecration of sacred places ; but there is an interesting tradition of a tribe which determined to accept Mbasi as God, contrary to the decision of the other tribes, and was severely defeated in battle ; and Mbasi, about whom more will be said in another chapter, has ever since been regarded as a deceiver. If there is anything in the tradition, it indicates a certain amount of loose cohesion among the tribes.

Approaching war was foretold by prophecy and by portent. The *abakunguluka* (prophets) declared that for the sins of the people war was coming ; the same terror was foretokened if the horns of the new moon were not of equal length, or if the cattle bellowed at night without obvious cause. But when a chief wished to go to war he held secret council with his headmen and official advisers, the objective of the war being almost always to "eat" the cattle of another chief. Usually it was agreed literally to sleep upon it. If one of the dreamers had a war-dream, as he might very well have, he told the others, and all together went to inform the chief. In these dreams, the progress of the fight was foreseen, and the result, including the individuals killed, was told to the chief. If the dream was favourable, confirmation was sought. The chief took his zebra tail of office, poured oil into it, and hung it up in the house of his chief wife. If during the night it exuded cattle dung and blood, the sign was good ; if blood only, it was bad. Blood indicated the death of men, but that was of secondary importance if the dung was there which indicated spoil in cattle as the result of victory. Along with the tail was hung up the chief's spear, which now gleamed and glittered like fire in the night, while the tail moved about with a swishing sound, indicating that the spirits urged battle. All this took place in the presence of the chief and the principal medicine man only ; and their report was published in the morning, when the blowing of a horn summoned all males to the meeting-place. " My children," says the chief, " we are hungry. Let us eat the cattle of so and so." But he gives the name, not of the real point of attack, but of some other chief living in another direction ; for there was always the possibility of traitors in the community, who would carry warning to the enemy.

A wild scene of hurry followed. Spears were collected and sharpened, defects attended to, new hafts attached. The shields were examined and strengthened if necessary. If there was a blacksmith in the village he was besieged by warriors whose weapons had become rusty or useless, all eager to equip themselves for the spoil. But man and weapon are alike useless until they have been given power and protection by the medicine man; and the armed warriors, standing in rows or circles, were sprinkled with medicine from a huge pot, rendering them and their weapons irresistible. In the rising of 1906 in the Songea area, it is said that the fighting men were so confident of the power of the drugs that they rushed up to the mouths of the German guns, only to perish there by the bullets which they believed would be turned into water.

Besides the publicly administered medicine, a more powerful drug was to be had for a fee; and the chief himself was armed and protected at all points in this way. One medicine ensured that his spear would find the heart of an enemy; another that the enemy's spear would fall short; a third he chewed as the fight went on; and a few very great chiefs possess a medicine which enables them to remove a fatal wound to a non-fatal spot. Those who could obtain it attached another medicine to the spear handle, and some carried a charm on their shields.

Fighting men carried spears numbering from six up to twenty; and the greater the number the bolder the hero, for a large number of spears indicated a determination not to run until every weapon available had been thrown at the enemy, or otherwise disposed of. Great heroes were followed by slaves who carried additional supplies of weapons. Some had wide shields of ox-hide, and others had narrow strips strengthened by slim bamboos. On their heads they wore the *ikipuhili*, a plume of red and black feathers, the capture of which from an enemy was the great ambition of every warrior. Arms, legs, and waist were partially covered by strips of hide with the hair attached, but these were meant to give a wild appearance, not to protect the body.

No man went out to battle with an unsettled quarrel hanging over him; the ancestors of the other party to the quarrel would see to it that he did not return. And the chief must be free from offence. One who proposed to go to war with other men's wives on his conscience, was sternly told by his councillors that his conduct made victory impossible, and he must make such amends as the law demanded. Except in cases of hurried attacks, such as the march of Munsoso to avenge an insult, all household fires were extinguished, and new fire obtained by rubbing. The women threw away their old bark-cloths, and used new ones. Just before setting out the chief went to the house of his first wife and prayed to his ancestors to grant him success. The war dance which followed the sprinkling with medicine might last for two or three days, and finally, armed and protected by weapons, medicines, prayers, and a good conscience, the warriors went forth.

The fighting began when the opposing forces came within a spear's throw of each other. Here and there a great hero stood out to hurl insulting language at the enemy, challenging them to " come on," and be scattered by his single arm. When the fighting became close, stabbing took the place of throwing, and if a very few were killed on either side, the losing side retired. But only for a short distance; for a hero stood out, and called the others to rally round him, and a few desperate men would drive back the enemy. And so the battle swayed to and fro, until one chief considered that his men had had enough, and made his submission ; or perhaps the fight was renewed next day when the tired men had rested. But so long as the chief went on blowing his *isiba* (usually a small horn), the battle went on. The great war horn was blown continuously, and the *ililonge*, a bamboo whistle with a penetrating note, made itself heard above the din.

Behind the fighting-line were the old men, one of whom held the *lusero*, a basket with a great selection of powerful medicines, very sacred, and of vital importance. If it was taken by the enemy, it was hoisted up for all to see, and if it was finally held by them, the dynasty to which it originally belonged died out. It was shaken by the old man who held it, and was carried forward or drawn back, according as the enemy retired or advanced. If the chief was an old man he did not enter the battle, but took his place in the rear, praying ; if he was defending his home, he prayed to God and to the spirits ; if he was the aggressor, he left out the prayer to the Deity !

After the men went out to fight, the women sat silent and unwashed in the villages until they returned, carefully avoiding quarrels, which would kill the husbands of the participants. They were stripped quite naked, " to give lightness of foot " in case the enemy forced an entrance. Women were never killed in war, for the victors were enriched with the cattle that went to redeem all captured wives or daughters. Nor were they taken as wives by the victors, although there is at least one well-known case where a woman was the sole objective of a war.

The dead might be buried where they fell, or brought home. The return of the host was awaited by the women in silence if the result of the fighting was not known to them. Each wife or mother recognized husband or son among the returning brave, but if one was told that her husband was coming on behind in another company, she knew that he was dead, and that his body was being brought home. If all returned in safety, and that sometimes happened in these far from desperate encounters, the women and girls set up their shrill cry, as exciting to an African as the pibroch to a Scot, and ran alongside, clapping and shouting in joy. The night was given up to feasting. The captured cattle were divided by the chief, lions' shares going to those who distinguished themselves in the fighting. The defeated chief, if he had any cattle left, also gave his men a feast, for they must not be allowed to lose heart over a single failure, and no doubt there was much boasting on both sides. If the sacred *lusero* with its medicines was taken from the enemy, it was put into the house in which the victorious chief kept his *ifingira*, the very powerful medicines by which his authority was (and is) upheld.

Cowards were held in supreme contempt. But a coward is not a man who runs away ; all do that as the struggle sways to and fro ; a coward is a man who does not enter the battle at all, but hangs in the rear with the old men, afraid to take his part in the fight ; or who fails to answer the rallying cry and help to turn the tide of battle. Tokens of contempt were heaped upon him. He got no share of the spoils. When the feast was going on, a piece of roasted flesh was handed to him on the burned end of a stick taken out of the fire ; if he dropped it he was beaten, the final disgrace. In very bad cases, his house was pulled down and his wives given to other men. But one who was ordered by the chief to keep out of the battle was not disgraced in this way. He did what he was told.

The spoils of war, which were practically always cattle, belonged to the chief. If a man captured ten head, the chief might give him back five or less according to favour or valour. From a headman he would take only one or two ; and out of all that fell to him he gave rewards to those who had distinguished themselves in the fighting, but had not taken cattle. No prisoners were taken, and the seriously wounded were killed. To let them live was to increase the number of future enemies, and to gain a reputation for softness which did not make for security against attacks from other quarters. And yet there was a pleasant kindness too ; a man who had a friend killed on the other side went freely to the enemy's country to mourn for him, and no one thought of molesting him. The frightful orgies of slaughter in which it would appear that some Bantu tribes indulge, are unknown in Konde warfare. The interminable death-roll of the Great War was a terrifying revelation of the unyielding nature of the Europeans in a quarrel.

Individual chiefs had special methods of securing victory. Mwamakula's wife, when her husband marched out with his forces, sat on a live sheep as long as the fighting went on: so assuring good luck to her husband in taking cattle, and preventing them running away when taken. Another wife sat on a cooking pot, to keep the enemy in a state of security while the warriors were closing in on them. They would go about as usual, unaware of danger, cooking and eating, until the storm burst, and there was no hope of defence. His sister had a *lusero* similar to the one carried into battle; and one of his old men lay down on the path, each soldier stepping over him as he passed on. While the fight was being waged, this old man sat on his haunches and pulled himself forward in that position, the effect being to make the enemy run. The *lusero* was carried hereditarily by Mfwimi, and when he laid it down it moved forward of itself as the enemy retired.

In the north there was a great prophet, whose presence in the battle always assured the victory to his own side; but if he retired, even for a moment, the battle turned, and he was brought back, by force if necessary.

Two great wars still stand out in the minds of the people: the victorious march of the Angoni, and the slaving invasion of the so-called Arabs. Both these enemies brought with them methods of fighting unknown to the Konde, who fled before the Angoni,

driving cattle and carrying what they could carry :
men and women flying naked for greater swiftness :
until the great Sango chief Merere, who is said to have
had three hundred guns, inflicted a severe defeat on
the invaders. After that the Konde made a few
feeble attempts to stand, but they came to nothing,
and the Angoni passed like a scourge through the
land. Against the Arabs a better fight was made, but
it was with the help of the white men who at that
time began to enter the Konde country.

The Konde were and are a timid people. The terror
of the Arabs has passed, but the fear of the Angoni
is probably a present fact. In August, 1914, some of
the leading men at Karonga came to me. " All you
white men," they said, " will be summoned to fight
in your own country, and we shall be left without
protection from the Angoni." I tried to reassure
them, but without success. " No," they said, " three
days after you go they will be upon us, and take away
all our cattle as they did before." Possibly a more
courageous spirit now obtains. A band of Angoni
were enlisted for special work at Karonga in the early
months of the war, and showed themselves so averse
from anything like danger, that the reputation of the
whole tribe, quite undeservedly, went down to zero.
" The fear of the Angoni," said some Konde to me at
that time, " is gone. If they were to come upon us
now, we would fight them." But it may be doubted
whether any but a few have really lost their old fears.

The Konde were never organized for war, and there
was no military caste. Everything connected with

A KONDE HUT.

Leisureliness is the key note of Konde life, and there is always time to sit down for the welcome chat about cattle, crops, children, or the white man, whose strange ways are of unfailing interest.

LION HUNTING.

The presence of a lion in a district causes a great scare, and the chief may call up all able-bodied men, armed with spears, clubs and bows, to the hunt. The lion—or leopard—is sometimes seized alive and clubbed or speared to death. The presence of a white man with a rifle gives increased courage to the hunters.

war was haphazard, or nearly so. Mostly a sudden rush to arms of untrained and unprepared men, with not even, in the less important cases, a declaration of war; though in the more important outbreaks a broken spear was sent as a token of hostility. This was the first intimation the Germans had in 1897 that the lake-shore chiefs were determined to fight. Such training as the men had was gained in the open-air sports of the cattle-tending stage; running (a very important accomplishment for a Konde warrior), leaping, spear throwing and stabbing. The only idea of formation was the straight, or rather straggling, line; the only conception of strategy was the sudden night or early morning attack. The man best pre-pared for battle was the man who had the greatest variety of medicines in or on him; nor can there be any doubt that these protective drugs and charms gave a sense of security which in turn generated a very real courage. Like so many other Bantu tribes, the Konde are a pastoral and agricultural community, so untrained in the arts of war that they did not even have stockades for protection, so common among most of their neighbours. The idea of a standing organization for defence or attack did not rise above their mental horizon, and when war came a wild rush to arms was their only resort.

M

CHAPTER XIV

The Supreme Being

OF the Supreme Being there is little that can be said with certainty beyond that He was believed in prior to the coming of the white man and the teachings of Christianity. The existence of this belief cannot be doubted. Indications of it are found everywhere in the native mind inextricably intertwined with life and thought and language, with prayer and sacrifice, with birth and death, with famine and pestilence and sword. For the rest, there is much confusion. That a developed theology does not exist, hardly needs to be said. What one informant will give as common belief, another will say he never heard of; it belongs, he will tell you, to another district, but it was not the belief of his fathers.

Many parables and proverbs, of the pre-European origin of which there can be no doubt, give evidence of the belief in a Supreme Being. "Who mocks at orphans," says an old proverb, "let him beware: God is watching him." "God will judge between us and the white man," a common saying at funerals, is necessarily of recent origin; but there are scores of other sayings which are certainly ancient. Many of these are expressed in archaic language, which is not in use at all to-day, except in these and similar sayings. Thus we have, " *Chikulu ku nsi*," the Great One is everywhere ; " *Gwende munono*," go where you will (you will hear of God). " *Imbwa yikurwa pa lwigi*," literally means, the dog is fighting at the door, but the actual meaning is, God is within you. Expressions like these are very numerous, and, even in their archaic form, are in common use every day.

The names in use for the Deity give some indication of how He is regarded. The name most commonly used in Konde is *Kyala*, but although it is now almost exclusively used in public worship, in the translation of the Scriptures, and in hymns, it is, perhaps, the weakest of all the Divine names. For it may be applied to persons in whom the Deity dwells, or to men who, though they lived on earth, were yet *Kyala*. The name is sometimes applied to white men, who are dangerous because they are believed to have closer relations with the source of all power than common men have. Other names are *Tenende*, the Owner of all things ; *Nkurumuke*, the Undying One ; *Chata*, the Originator ; *Kyaubiri*, the Unseen ; *Kalesi*, He who is everywhere present. The name *Ndorombwike* is the one used on solemn occasions, and comes from the verb *kutoromboka*, to create in a sense in which God only can. *Mperi*, again, is the Maker, applied to God only, though the verb from which it is derived may be applied to men also.

Prayer is addressed directly to the ancestral spirits, who in many cases are conceived as having power of themselves to grant a petition ; but more frequently they are entreated to carry the petitions to God, who alone can give what is asked for. " Why do you ask me for rain ? " says Chungu, when his impatient people come to him, " God owns the rain, and only He can give it." " But," reply the people, " common men cannot pray. Pray you to your ancestors, and let them carry your prayer to God." There is, however, also direct address in the formula, "Be gracious to us, O God, and hear the prayers of those whom we have named," the reference being to the spirits, to whom the main body of the petition is addressed. At birth, prayer is offered for the welfare of the child, " May God be gracious to you, my son." The dead are with God, and the spirits who were in the underworld before the entrance there of the souls of men, see His face, " for these are they who see God." Sickness also may be a divine infliction, though it may also be due to the wrath of an offended spirit. A heathen chief who came to see me during an illness, said, " You will recover if it is God's will," words which might well be a mere echo of what he had heard from Christian teachers ; but the impression they made on me was that he was expressing a pious thought from the depths of his own being.

When I was told that Chungu had once crossed the lake on dry land, and asked how that could be, the answer, quietly and seriously given, was that " Chungu is the man who speaks with God " ; why therefore should the statement be doubted ? God gives to prophets their dream-visions, and to others their inspired moments. He is the Maker of sorcerers as well as of common people. " Why do you kill me ? " demanded an agonized sorcerer from within the house where they were burning him to death. " Did God not make me as well as you ? " " Yes," was the grim reply, " but He also made the grass we burn in November."

The Supreme Being reveals Himself " in divers manners." What is specially great of its kind ; a great ox, or even a he-goat ; a very big tree, or any other specially impressive object, is called *Kyala*, by which is probably meant that God takes up a temporary abode in them. In a great storm God is walking on the lake. A waterfall, when it is unusually noisy, is His voice. In 1921 God called from a waterfall in the Nserya district during the night, and the message, interpreted by the *abakomwa malago* (inspired persons), was that all must die because of the evil that was rampant in the district. The earthquake is His mighty footstep, and the lightning is *Lesa*, God coming down in anger, when all rational people sit silent or speak in whispers, lest " the anger," hearing them, should smite them down. He sometimes comes in the body of a lion or a snake, and in such a form " He walks among men to see their doings."

He is a God of righteousness, though the Konde idea of righteousness does not always coincide with ours. Unrighteousness is an offence against God, even though they do not always know why, and He never comes except when evil is prevalent, and punishment is needed, a point of view from which it is easy to understand that the chief desire of the people is to induce Him to go away again. " Go far hence, O God, to the Sango, for Thy House is very large," is a prayer which is not seldom heard, when it is believed that He is near. An eclipse is a special visitation, and is met with wild drumming and shouting, confession of sins, and entreaties, for the consciousness of sin is by no means absent from their minds. Offerings are brought to the spirits to induce them to intercede, but no offerings are made to *Ndorombwike* Himself, for nothing can be offered that has any value for Him. " God is calling in the waterfall," " God has kindled a fire in the pool," are cries of dread alarm to this day, only in a small degree comparable to the fear that is inspired when it is declared that a spirit, of however great a man, is angry. God is an ever present terror, and the idea of communion with Him for any purpose, is one that has not entered the Konde mind. He is *Tenende*, the Owner of the world, and it is for men to see that He is not offended. Of the many sins which bring the wrath of God and the spirits on the community, the most important are widespread sexual sin, and neglect of sacrifices.

And yet God is *Tata Twesa*, the Father of us all, from whom help may be expected when men deserve it. The remarkable incident of the floating of the *Domira*, referred to in Chapter I, bears its own evidence of native thinking about the Deity. " Then I said, Rejoice, for God has heard my prayers." It does not seem open to reasonable doubt that Chungu was casting himself upon unseen powers, making, in fact, what Christians call the venture of faith; and his men, believing that he was in touch with God, knew that he could give additional strength to their arms, and they pulled successfully.

Nevertheless, it is important to guard against exaggerated ideas of the Supreme Being as He is conceived by the Konde. It is not to be supposed that the African idea of Omnipotence has much in common with the Christian and Philosophic ideas on the subject. God is a magnified human being, a being anthropomorphically conceived. Omnipotence is an idea limited by the native capacity to conceive of powers beyond power to do without limit what he himself can do within limits. The vastness of time and space, and the illimitable forces acting throughout the universe, are unrepresented in the native mind, and therefore the conception of a Supreme Being is severely limited. But the point is, that such as He is, He is supreme over men and spirits, and over the forces of Nature as these are understood; and that is sufficient in the minds of the Konde, as it is sufficient in the minds of more highly developed peoples, to place God in a category by Himself, in a position which He shares with no other being.

Do the Konde recognize minor deities? The question is not easy to answer. An old man with whom I was conversing on the subject recently, looked at me with surprise when I brought the conversation round to " other gods." " There is only one *Kyala* (God)," he said with great emphasis, and other old men gave the same decided reply; nor do the younger men admit that their fathers ever acknowledged more than one God. And yet, as I have already indicated, the name *Kyala* is by no means restricted to the Supreme Being; and there are legends of human gods which go far back into the past. The Henga, a neighbouring tribe, freely acknowledge the worship, in the past, of a number of minor deities, and belief in them is common among the Bantu peoples generally. This is, perhaps, the point at which the confusion in the Konde mind reveals itself most decidedly, for it is the border line between the spirits of great chiefs still active in the underworld, minor deities, and the Supreme Being Himself.

In the land of Marongo, from which the Konde originally came, so say the fathers (who in the same breath will deny the existence of more than one God), there were three gods, *Lyambilo*, *Mbasi*, and *Ngeketo*. Of *Lyambilo* all that need be said is that he is still the god of the Kinga. *Ngeketo* was the youngest of the three, and one day he went with his boy friends to herd the cattle on the plain. While they were there *Ngeketo* took maize and planted it, and lo! it grew, and the same day they ate it roasted in the fire. When the elders of the people and the other two gods heard of it, they were jealous and slew *Ngeketo*. He lay dead for three days, and on the third day he arose, but was killed again in exceeding great anger. Again he arose, and was seen by some, but disappeared, and it was said that he went to the coast, where he became the God of the white man. The older men say that this story has not been modified by Christian influence and it may be so, but there is a variant, which is free from suspicion, in which the God came back to life in the form of a serpent, was cut to pieces by his fellow-gods and the elders, who, when he again came back, served him as before, upon which he went to the white man, who to this day prays to him. At Karonga the old people used to say, " We have smitten the Son of God in the neck," but I have not been able to trace the origin or connection of the saying, except that it is not Christian, and may be connected with traditions of *Ngeketo*.

The story of *Mbasi* is very different. He is the evil one, to whom deceit and wickedness are a pleasure. Europeans are still living who have seen the great stores of ivory and cloth which were offered to him by terror-inspired people, and laid up in a cave at Matema on the lake shore. The cave has now been robbed of its contents, as *Mbasi* himself has been of whatever of dread his name inspired in the past. It is not very long ago that the last prophet of *Mbasi* died. He lived near Masoko, and within living memory he climbed a small eminence there, and proclaimed that *Mbasi* demanded cattle to be sent to him without delay, the prophet himself being the guardian appointed by the God. And the cattle were sent in goodly numbers !

Long ago, says a legend, when *Mbasi* walked the earth, he had men who were always with him. Mwasómola went with him to his friend Mwakanya-mata. *Mbasi* told them many things, of witchcraft, of hunger, of diseases that were to come, of the approach of the Angoni warriors, and where to flee for safety when they arrived. He asked for *bhang* and a pipe, and these were laid on the ground, and soon smoke was seen issuing from the earth. For *Mbasi* was not seen ; they only heard his voice. Then he became communicative. " The Angoni are coming now," he told them, " go at once to Masoko with your wives and children and cattle." The unfortunate Mwakanyamata did as he was advised, only to be robbed of all his cattle by another friend of *Mbasi*, to whom the deceitful God sent word to have no mercy on the cattle of a fool like Mwakanyamata, who believed what he was told! And to this day Mwakanyamata is laughed at as the man who allowed himself to be deceived by the wiles of *Mbasi*.

According to another version, *Mbasi* was a rival claimant to Divine honours with *Ndorombwike* Himself. Originally he was a serpent, killed in the dim past by the chief Mwakibinga. *Mbasi* returned to earth as a spirit, seeking to persuade men to worship him, offering them wealth in cattle if they agreed. But men refused, " for the dead do not return." One chief, Mwatonoka, accepted the false God, but was defeated in battle by Mwakarobo, a final proof that *Mbasi* was a deceiver.

Stories of *Mbasi* and his activities are numerous. He used to do some of his own work ; that is to say, instead of sending one of his prophets to demand what he wanted, he shouted from the great *ilisyeto* (grave of a chief ; place of prayer) at Lubaga in Nserya, and made his own demands. Milk, beer, bananas, were placed at the door of Mwakindingo his prophet, and if in the morning the quantity was found to be less, it was clear to all that *Mbasi* had come to receive the offerings.

But the trick worked too often. As the fear of *Mbasi* diminished, men began to take advantage of their still credulous neighbours, and to demand in the name of the fading divinity cattle, beer, food supplies, to be sent to the places indicated by the impersonator of the God. This became so common that the Germans, who then ruled the country, interfered and put it down.

Very long ago there lived near Karonga a man called Firaguli, who after his death became a godlet, and lived on the mountain which now goes by his name. There was also a great man called Kambwe, who entered the ranks of the gods or godlets at his death, and lived in the pool a few miles from Karonga, to which in like manner he has given his name. To both of these divinities the people prayed in long-past times; and both, though able to see to the general welfare of the people, were not strong enough to punish them when evil was prevalent. When punishment was necessary, they called in the help of Mwanjebe, a minor deity of the neighbouring Henga people. Firaguli went south on a favouring breeze to invite his more powerful neighbour to come to his help; and Mwanjebe, who lived in a pool at the foot of a waterfall near the Overtoun Institution, came up on a floating island. Then smallpox broke out among the people, and if a visit to Kambwe showed that the pool was bubbling, it was evident that Mwanjebe was there, and must be got rid of as soon as possible. Prayers and promises of repentance were offered, and if that did not satisfy the god, more drastic measures were taken. A great stone was heated and tumbled into the pool, around which gathered a great multitude of people, stabbing fiercely at the water with spears and reeds, to drive off the unwelcome deity. The cessation of the bubbling showed that he had gone, and the fact was still further proved when the smallpox ceased. All three godlets are now mere memories, and, except as memories, they have completely vanished, leaving the field clear for the ancestral spirits and the Supreme Being.

There was in the worship, if indeed a determined effort to drive off the deity could be called worship, " no stimulus to the realization of the riches which are given to man in his own nature." The gods presented no problems, for all problems were solved long ago by the fathers ; and hence man's relation to them contained nothing upon which the faculties might work and be developed. The religion was stagnant, and the people were stagnant with it.

There was no art ; not even rude representations of the gods ; no poetry arising out of a feeling of devotion, for devotion there was none. In the case of the godlets I have mentioned, even the qualities which caused them to take rank as gods after death have been forgotten. It may be that the stories of " the brave days of old," to be related in a later chapter, afford us a hint of how the process of deification, now probably at an end for ever, went on in the past. But the Konde, in common with all Bantu peoples, made the great transition from a vague ill-conceived " power behind an object or an act, to the free being conceived with human attributes and feelings," who can interfere in the affairs of the community, even if it be also true that such gods roused themselves into activity only when evil demanded punishment, remaining quiescent except under such stimulus.

CHAPTER XV

The Ancestral Spirits

THE importance of the spirits in the everyday life of the Konde can hardly be over-estimated. From the day that the month-old infant is presented by the head of the family to the spirits of its ancestors—though this ceremony is dying out at Karonga—until the day of death, when the spirit is directed to go in peace and confidence to meet his forefathers, living and dead are mingled in one stream of life, form one community, and are dependent upon each other for many of the best things "above" on earth here, and "below" where the spirits are. Yet it is by no means easy to define the relation of the living man to the spirits of his fathers who are ever about him. It is, perhaps with more facility than the facts warrant, usually defined as an attitude of worship; but there are at least indications that the attitude is incompletely expressed by the idea of worship.

Sacrifices, or offerings, are made to the spirits; and this, it need not be doubted, is an act of worship. The word used is *ukwikemesya*, which is used by British and German missionaries to denote an act of worship offered to God. On the other hand, the food, beer, and other things placed at the graves, are intended to maintain in some way the life of the spirits, to keep them in countenance in their own world. For as men are dependent on the goodwill of the spirits for the best things of life, so do the spirits depend upon their descendants on earth for much of what they require in the other world.

The dead are conceived as obtaining a great access of power on passing into the spirit world, power for good or evil, and to placate them is one of the chief preoccupations of Konde life. But while it would not be true to say that compulsion can be brought to bear upon the spirits, that once the appropriate ceremonies are performed, the spirit must fulfil the prayer of the petitioners, yet so complete is the faith of the common man in the power of these ceremonies, that it may be suggested that prayer and answer are inseparably bound up together ; if compulsion is too strong a word, obligation, if milder, is perhaps sufficient.

The spirits are called *basyuka*. The verb *kusyuka* means to rise from the dead, to resume ordinary bodily activities ; but the noun formed from this verb, *unsyuka* (of which the plural is *basyuka*), means the inner man, the life of which is independent of the body. Now when the *unsyuka* leaves the body, it does not die, it goes to *ubusyuka*, the land of spirits, where in all respects except that of having a body, it retains its humanity. The spirits are not, however, called *abandu* men ; though the related term *imindu*, which, applied to living men, is an insult, is often given to them. There is no conception more firmly fixed in the Konde mind than that " the dead do not return " ; they do not resume earthly life in bodily form ; though they do return in spirit form, and sometimes exert themselves very energetically. The dead are with God : this is a conviction so universal that it cannot be the result of Christian teaching. And God is not above, as in our cosmology, but below. *"Kumwanya kuno malabasya,"* is a frequent expression on the lips of some people. *Kwirabasya* means to be idle when one might be working ; and the meaning of the phrase is that man's permanent home is not " above " on earth, but " below," very much as in the statement of St. Paul, " our citizenship is in heaven."

At death, or rather at burial, the head of the family, calling for silence from the wailing women, addresses the spirits by name, praying them to receive their friend. Then addressing the dead man directly, he says :

" And you, friend, go to the land of spirits. Go in peace. Go to meet all whom we have named. They will recognize you. Salute them all. Tell them that we are paying taxes, that those men are an affliction to us. It was not we who killed you. Nay, we weep for your death."

The words, " these men are affliction to us," refer to the Europeans, and are still in use, though of recent years they have been gradually dropping out of the valedictory address at the grave. Another expression still sometimes used, is " God will judge between us and the white man," a clear indication that the white man is not received everywhere as an unmixed blessing.

The entrance to the spirit world is the grave ; and all that is done there is intended to give the dead man a favourable entrance upon his new state ; well dressed, well supplied with all the necessaries of life ; for he goes to God. The conditions of life below are the same as those above. The chief is a chief still, and the slave a slave. The rich man continues to be rich, and the poor goes on in his poverty. The wife goes to her husband, children to their parents. There is no retribution, no righting of wrongs. The judgment of God against the white man will be manifested here on earth, not in the future state. The unmarried man remains unmarried, and his body is smeared with charcoal, so that he may not, on arrival, be mistaken for a married man. Cattle are there, but they need no tending ; bananas, but they require no cultivation. There is bush for the hunter, and streams for the fisher. But everything is small: cattle, houses, crops, even the spirits themselves, are *sekere*, thin, unsubstantial.

Prior to the arrival of the first human spirits, the place was inhabited by the owners of the land ; and " these are they who see God, for God is a Spirit." Therefore human beings going there are strangers, but are well received, and given all necessaries, including land.

Although the dwelling of the spirits is below, they

N

are by no means confined to that region, but come up frequently, especially at night, when they sit on the graves and chat, or go to the houses of their descendants seeking food or beer, and to assure themselves that there is still a "fire" there, and fire means descendants. In the house they make a noise, *hu, hu, hu,* heard by the people within, and morning reveals soiled food and beer grown thick, evidence that cannot be gainsaid of a spirit-visitor. Spirits are sometimes visible, but if addressed by name they will disappear. They cannot be seen in bright moonlight, and fire renders them invisible : a fireless house at night is still a terror to little children. A visit from a spirit is most unwelcome, especially to women and children, though the men claim that they are not afraid. Specially terrifying is a recently dead person who has been buried near the house. *"Pasisya panja"* (there is terror outside) they say on a dark night, for the spirit of the dead man may be sitting on the mound which marks his grave. No one willingly passes the grave of a dead chief at night, for one may hear his name called ; then woe to the man who looks behind, for he will die ; or if he hears his name, but has the will not to look, some lesser evil will overtake him.

Wood noises in a wind, the moaning of the trees, is the voice of a spirit in the tree. If a branch snaps, and the passer-by looks round, evil will come ; and if his name is called it is a sign that " his number is up," he has not long to live. But it may happen that the snapping of the branch is quite harmless, being merely intended to make him look round, so that the spirit may get a good view of him, and see if he is his " child."

The spirits return to earth for many reasons, but chiefly for two. The first is to assure themselves that they still have descendants on earth ; for if the family dies out it is a dreadful calamity for the ghosts : they become frogs. The second reason is to make sure that they are not forgotten by the living, for the spirit to whom no attention is paid by the living becomes of no account in the underworld. Hence the illness or other misfortune which overtakes the living ; stern reminder of duty to the dead, who will not permit neglect.

By night the spirits, when they are visible at all, take human form ; but by day they come in the form of birds, serpents, lions ; and they come as small red or black ants to eat the flesh offered in sacrifice at the grave of a chief. When the spirit takes the form of a serpent, he is testing the loyalty of his descendants : if they try to kill him, it is a bad sign ; they ought to know who it is, for such " occupied " snakes never bite anyone. Only chiefs enter into lions, going about to see how the people are behaving. God Himself also comes in this form, and for the same reason ; and the lion, like the serpent, is harmless. The idea, common in some parts of Bantu Africa, that a child who resembles his dead grandfather is that grandfather come back to life, is scoffed at by the Konde. The child is like his grandfather, and that is all.

Of the persons officially connected with the spirits, the most important is the chief. It has already been said that " Chungu is the man who speaks with God " ; he is also the man who speaks with authority to the spirits. He, and all other chiefs, approach the spirits for the general good, but as heads of families they have the right to offer private prayers as well. Each head of a family may also pray for his own people ; but no man may pray so long as his father or elder brother is alive. Next, every chief has an official who may be called a priest ; he is the *unnyago*, the man whose duty it is to go daily at the order of the chief to present an offering at the grave where the last chief is buried. He does not pray ; he simply lays the offering, usually a few maize cobs, on the grave and departs. When the chief goes in person to pray, as he sometimes does, without any public ceremony, this man goes with him, hears the prayers, and knows the ritual ; and it is he who will teach the new chief his duties when the time comes for him to perform them. When, however, the chief dies, the *unnyago* is in great danger, for the spirits take possession of his person, a danger which can only be averted by a powerful medicine supplied by the doctor, and taken as soon as the chief has died. If this is not done, he becomes mad, lives in the bush, gibbering and naming all the dead chiefs of the past, including names known to no living person, but supposed to be those of long-dead chiefs, uttered by themselves through him.

With regard to places of worship : the " high place " is always at the grave of the dead chief ; and it is there that prayer for the community at large is offered by the living chief. All over the land there are more or less important graves, where local chiefs pray with their people; but the most important is naturally the one at Mphande, near Karonga, where Chungu goes to pray. At the house of every head of a family there is the *ikiyinja*, the sacred banana grove, where the family ceremonies are performed. This grove is never cut down, and the wife must not eat the fruit of it, for the spirit of her father-in-law is there if he is dead; if not, of ancestral fathers-in-law. The decay of the spirit hut, a small erection covering the grave of a chief, is attended with great danger to all the people, for the dead chief will some day visit his resentment upon his unworthy successor, whose duty it is to keep the hut in order; and when the chief suffers, his land suffers with him. A sheep or goat is tied up at the place, and if it is found there in the morning, all is well, it is killed, and the hut is re-built. But if it has been killed by some prowling beast of prey, the dead chief is very angry, and the diviner must say what else must be done to appease him, before another animal is found for the sacrifice, and the hut rebuilt.

Here and there are to be found traces of non-human spirits. They are not called *basyuka*, but *mapiri*, a word which in the neighbouring Henga dialect means hills, but the Konde use it in invocation when crossing water. Their dwelling is in the water; and they are pre-human, spirits that were in the world when the whole earth was covered with water. When, later, men came, more favoured of God, the waters retired to the lakes and pools, and there these spirits exist to this day, at enmity with men, whom they seek to destroy. On the lake, during a storm, they are still to be heard, demanding a victim to be thrown to them whom they may " eat." In the past, if a canoe was overtaken by a storm, one of the rowers was thrown into the water, whereupon the storm ceased, and the others arrived in safety.

At many places all over the district there are pools in which these spirits dwell. The most interesting is at Kisyombe, and about it many stories are told, and believed, which throw an interesting light on the Konde mind. When the chief of three generations ago was a very old man, it was prophesied that at his death the lake would recede, the fish would die, bush would grow where water was, and a great disease would carry off many of the people. And it all happened. But the lake, as it receded, left a pool in which some spirits were imprisoned. It is now partly silted up with sand, and treacherous to walk upon. If a man finds himself sinking as he walks over it, he calls out that he belongs to Kisyombe, whereupon he is pushed up from below by the water-spirits, who own Kisyombe's power. A boy who sank right through, but was returned, was directed by the spirits to give a report of all that he saw, and particularly he must insist that these spirits are *abandu* (human beings). If no sacrifice is offered the spirits take their due, by snatching at passing children ; but it is long since the last child was taken. The pool at Rungwe is distinguished for the drastic action of the people, who, exasperated by the frequent disappearance of children, tumbled an immense heated stone into the pool, and so drove out the spirits, who to this day dwell in a pool in the Sango country, " where the white men go to see them."

Yet another class are the mountain or hill spirits. Offerings are made to them by people climbing steep hill-sides. A stone is picked up, breathed upon, and laid upon a large flat stone, or in the fork of a tree, with the prayer, " May my feet be light." These stones are to be seen to-day in small heaps on many a steep ascent. Sometimes more valuable offerings were made, though these have now ceased. A fowl, a sheep, or a goat, was brought, and left alive to meet whatever fate might be in store for it. These spirits, like those of the water, are pre-human, and hostile to mankind, upon whom they bring many diseases. Belief in them is dying out, and the younger people know little or nothing about them.

CHAPTER XVI

The Worship of the Spirits

THE Konde are either a deeply religious, or a deplorably spirit-ridden people; and, having regard to some of the prayers given in this chapter and throughout the book, I am inclined to think that religious is the more correct term. It is true that the prayers are in all cases for material goods, such as health and good fortune, for rain and crops, for protection against pestilence; but if religion means a sense of dependence upon unseen powers, then it cannot be denied that the Konde are religious.

On all great occasions, prayer and offerings are made; but also when a spirit is believed to be angry: if there is quarrelling in the family; if a man beats his wife; if a girl has arrived at puberty, or a marriage has been arranged, without their being consulted; if a woman has been unfaithful to her husband; if a man neglect his parents; if ceremonies are neglected; or the spirits themselves forgotten. Their wrath is shown very specially by a disease of the lips breaking out on the guilty person, and by fever; but also in many other ways; by the failure of the beer to ferment, by sickness, by a storm in which some one is drowned, by failure of crops, of increase of livestock, of children, by too little or too much rain, or by ill-success in hunting or fishing; and, very emphatically, by a sudden death.

The prayer and ceremony at the presentation of a new-born child have already been given. More pathetic is the prayer offered when a child is ill. Standing at the sacred banana grove, the family representative prays :

" . . . and now this little one whom I hold in my hands, be gracious to him. He [she] has come into a world of sickness, of cold, of all the troubles that you yourselves were familiar with. Let him lie in peace. Let none in the spirit-land be angry with him. To-morrow he will be full-grown, and he will bring you beer, flesh, flour. Pray to God for him. O God, who art Lord of all, let thy breath be cool upon him (liti, Let thy spittle be cool upon him)."

Then, spitting on the child's breast and back, he says :

"And thou child, may there be life in thee. God be gracious unto thee. Live in peace and be not wearied."

Not all diseases are due to the anger of the spirits ; a natural illness is one that yields to treatment. It is the act of God, and when the right medicine has been used, cure will follow, for God does not need to be entreated as the spirits do. Yet the spirits carry their petitions to God, as if He did need to be entreated, but the Konde see no contradiction there. If a diviner has to be consulted, the process is long, and the result not certain, at least at first. The omission of a name from the list of ancestors may cause delay, for the omitted one will refuse to go to God with the petition, and unanimity is of the very essence of prayer. Or, again, the wrong person may offer the prayer and offerings which follow upon discovery, by the diviner, of the offended spirit; this is so important that I have known a man go a hundred and forty miles to his elder brother, to have his prayers correctly offered.

The *umputi* (person who prays; the name is now applied to all clergymen) goes to the graveside, or he stands at the banana grove set apart for the purpose, or on the verandah of his house, and prays:

"My fathers, I have come to you because I have found that you have caused the illness of my friend. You are angry with him because he has given you no beer. Now the *malesi* (cereal from which beer is made) is here; behold it, all of you, with your eyes, and when it is made I will bring it to you and you shall be satisfied. Then let the sickness leave the body of our friend."

Then taking water into his mouth, he squirts it out, *pu* (*puta*, pray).

When the beer has been made, he goes again to pray:

"You, and you, and you [naming them], come to the feast. You who died by a crocodile, who

were killed by a tree, who were killed in war, by
lightning, by lion or leopard, I call you all to come ;
and whosoever has been forgotten, let him come.
I pray to you all, let my dog be well, let him lie
down in peace. He is the saliva of God. O God,
be merciful, and turn back the disease."

The beer that he brought and laid on the ground
before him, is now poured into the palms of little
children, who drink it in that way. If a flesh offering
is also made, it is laid down in small pieces, and each
ancestor is named as his portion is laid down. When
ants come out to feast on it, it is known that the
spirits have accepted the offering, and all present run
away lest the spirits should work evil upon them.

Little children are affectionately referred to as
dogs, especially when they commit a fault, which the
father apologizes for. " How can you be angry with
the little one ? He has no more sense of what is fitting
than a dog." But to call a person a dog in any other
connection is a great insult, and must be atoned for.
Spitting on a person is another insult, but when done
ceremonially, it is believed to have great virtue, and is
no doubt connected with the idea of the " Spittle of
God " referred to above.

If the sick person does not recover, the fault is not
in the system. Some mistake has been made, the
diviner is unskilful, his wife is " unclean," or some
other cause prevents the expected result from following ; for, when the proper ceremonies have been performed, the patient recovers. But a final cause of
failure is always kept in hand ; it is the will of God

that the sick man should die, and there is nothing more that can be done. Numerous instances have been cited to me of recovery of sick persons when all had been correctly performed ; and scepticism on the subject was received with almost incredulous amazement. And there is no reason to doubt that in many cases recovery did follow ; for the conviction in the mind of the patient that the wrath of the offended spirit had been averted, would, according to modern ideas of psychology, have a healing effect also upon his body.

Smallpox is the disease most dreaded by the people, and its approach was accompanied with most elaborate ceremonies. The subject is dealt with again under " Witchcraft " and " Medicine." It might come either through the action of the spirits or through witchcraft. In either case its approach is foreseen by the *abakunguluka* (prophets) in dreams, and the chief and his subordinates go to the grave of the ancestors, and there, by night, a black ram is killed. The lungs and liver are roasted, and laid in little heaps on the grave, each ancestor being named as his portion is laid down, and prayer is offered :

" Ye fathers, look upon us in mercy. Drive away from us this plague, lest our children die, and none be left in the land. Send it to the Basango or the Basafwa, but save us. Pray to God for us. Hear, O God, the words of those we have named. And go to the west, O God, or to the Basango."

The flesh is now eaten roasted, and the stomach of the animal, filled with medicines not known to me, is given to an old man, and the skin placed on his back; with these he goes, by night, through the whole district covered by the prayer. If the journey is not finished in one night, he lies in a village until it is dark again, care being taken that he is seen by none, and completes his circuit. On his return, the chief calls all the people together, and declares that if the disease is the work of witchcraft, the evil ones will certainly be discovered and punished; but if it is the work of the spirits, " we have prayed to them to send it far hence to the Basango." Family ceremonies, of a similar nature, follow, each head of a family offering a little beer to his ancestors. At Karonga this latter ceremony has almost entirely been abandoned. There, however, the prophet to whom the coming of smallpox has been revealed goes about the villages, crying, " *ilibofu, ilibofu, ilibofu* " (smell, of dead bodies), a dreadful cry, which brings the people in a mass to the chief to demand the performance of the ceremonies. Similar prayers are offered when mumps, dysentery, or widespread eye disease visits the community.

When a man is about to set out on a journey, his father gives him his blessing, and prays to the spirits for him, adding:

" May lion and leopard and hyena, crocodile and snake and falling tree, be far from you, and may you return in peace."

A person involved in a lawsuit was similarly prayed for :

> " Be merciful, and let his case be good. May he escape and return to us ; for those men are gods ; whom they imprison they imprison, and whom they kill they kill."

The men referred to are the European Administrative Officers, before whom cases are heard. If the case is tried by a native chief, the clause is omitted. A man who has been away at work, in the employment of a white man, gives, on his return in safety, a piece of cloth to the family representative, who, after it has been laid up in the house for a time, asks the permission of the spirits to wear it, for it is theirs ; and, taking their permission for granted, leaves a tiny rag to represent it. Less careful persons wear it at once, the rag being enough to keep the spirits in good temper. The numerous other occasions on which worship is offered are described in the appropriate chapters.

Greatest of all Konde ceremonies is the prayer for rain. And around this ceremony much erroneous information has collected ; for the so-called " rain-maker " does not make the rain ; his duties are quite different. The rain is the gift of God ; it is His to give or withhold as He sees fit. All that living men can do is to pray to the spirits, who, in turn, present the petition to God ; and God, if there is no obstacle among men themselves, will grant the petition.

Of sacred objects connected with rain ceremonies, the most important is the *mulima* (an old word meaning *the world*), which is never seen by anyone except its guardian, and very rarely even by him. It was originally in the possession of Chungu, but some generations ago was passed secretly by the reigning Chungu to a son who was hated by the people, and not in the least likely to succeed to royal dignity. It is at present guarded by a man called " Tom," though, fortunately perhaps, the honorific name of *Mwaka-banga* is used in direct address. As no one sees it, descriptions must be received with caution, and there are many natives who disbelieve in its existence, regarding the whole story as the invention of men who wished to gain honour for themselves. It is commonly described as about the size of a man's fist, with *maso* (eyes) all over it, of the size and colour of a red bean. When the eyes open, rain is coming, when they close it is being withheld. But, as the *mulima* is kept buried in the ground, it is not quite clear how it is known whether the eyes are closed or open. So long as the stone, if it is a stone, is kept in the ground rain will fall normally, but if the guardian has a quarrel with another chief, he will dig it up, a signal to the spirits that something is wrong, which must be dealt with before they go to God to ask for the rain.

Prayer for rain is offered, either when it becomes clear that " God's rain," that is to say, rain that comes without prayer, is not to fall ; or when the official dreamers declare that they do not see the rain where they always see it. Numerous variations in the actual words and ceremonies are found, almost every chief having some special form of his own ; but what is here given is obtained from descriptions by persons who were actually present at prayer offered by Chungu. The decision to pray does not originate with the chief himself; it comes from the people, who approach Chungu through the subordinate chiefs, and Chungu, after reminding them that only God can give rain, consents to pray.

In the past a human sacrifice was offered, and the flesh of the victim, burned and ground to powder, was distributed over the district as a "medicine" guaranteed to ensure a good crop. This has long ceased at Karonga; the last known occurrence of it farther north was in 1907, when a boy of about ten was sacrificed; and in 1917 a boy mysteriously disappeared, not without suspicion that he was offered in sacrifice. I have been told that human sacrifice is offered in the Kinga Mountains even now; but, except for repeated statements, I have no evidence. The victim, always a boy, is made to drink beer until he dies, when his body is burned and ground to powder for distribution. The child is selected in secret conclave by the chiefs, and no one knows that the tragedy has taken place until public announcement has been made, except the parents of the boy, whose disappearance must have been known to them. Weeping for the victim is prohibited.

For the ordinary sacrifice offered to-day, a black or white ox or cow, preferably the latter, has to be found, and brought to Chungu. The owner must be paid, and there is a case known where refusal to do so led to the failure of the whole ceremony. When the

IN THE KINGA MOUNTAINS (LIVINGSTONE RANGE.)

The cold is so great during part of the year, that the people sleep in pits, heated by fires which are extinguished at bedtime, and the openings carefully closed. Many of the little children emerging naked into the frosty morning air, die of pneumonia, and the pits are gradually being abandoned.

animal is found Chungu and his councillors go to the river to wash, and must not return to their wives until the whole ceremony is over. Arrived at the *ilisyeto* (burial place), the chief and those who are with him salute the dead by lying prone on their backs, then turning to the right, and finally assuming a sitting position, a soft hand-clapping accompanying these movements. Chungu then, sitting on the ground, and with his eyes open, addresses his ancestors :

" Hear me, ye who were before us [naming them]. I have brought this ox for the whole people. We cry to you. Why are you angry with us ? Why do you not go to God to pray for us ? Our children are dying. Pray for us. Thou who art not seen with the eyes of men, hear the petitions of those whom we name unto thee."

The animal is then killed by a blow on the back of the neck with an axe, and the flesh laid in little heaps upon the grave, each ancestor being named as his portion is laid down. The chief and his followers also feast until the ants come out and attack the portions laid down for the spirits, when all flee, for the spirits have come to accept the sacrifice, and it is well not to be too near them. For three days those who took part in the ceremony remain in their houses, for they have been in contact with unseen powers, and are dangerous until the effect has passed off. If the animal brought for sacrifice breaks its halter and gets away during the prayers, it is a token that something is wrong, and all proceedings are stayed until the wrong is discovered and righted.

o

Now begin the duties of the person who is called the rainmaker. In the Misuku Hills there is a rain forest, the trees of which drop moisture. Word is sent to the local chief that the spirits have accepted the prayers of Chungu ; and a quantity of rain-tree twigs is sent and delivered to the rainmaker. This official, known as the * unsusi*, goes to the lake by night to fetch water, which is placed in a pot along with the twigs, and some small smooth black or white stones, the pot being now covered with banana leaves, and placed near a small bush " where God stores the rain." The rainmaker now goes into his house, where he prays, lying on his face ; a position which he retains until rain has actually fallen. Chungu also continues in prayer.

The rainmaker is a quite inferior official. In the past he might be a slave, or any other unimportant person appointed for the duty. His function seems to be that of a " conductor," through whose person, or acts, or abstinence from action, the continuance of the rain granted at the prayer of the chief is assured. He must not cut his hair during the rainy season, for the heavens would dry up if he did. He must not wash in water, for that would bring on a flood ; in June he may begin cautiously to wash himself, and later he may indulge in the luxury of a full bath, and at the same time he may cut, but not shave, his hair. He must not be angry or scold during the rains, lest he bring on a lightning storm with fatal effects to some one. Further, during all those months he may not roast maize or ground-nuts, the leaping of which while being roasted is like the play of lightning, and would bring on a fatal stroke from the sky.

In 1912 " God's rain " fell as usual in December ; but in January came drought which continued into February. Urgent messages were sent to Chungu, who replied that he was helpless, as the *mulima* was lost. After diligent inquiry, it was found to be in possession of Mwandosya, who refused to act, because in the distribution of the cattle of a deceased relative another chief, Kasikula, had taken more than his share. Kasikula was ordered by Chungu to restore the balance, but he refused, and only agreed when the men present took up clubs to thrash him into obedience. Prayer was then offered in the usual way, and Mwandosya announced that God had commanded him to forgive the offender. " Rain," he said, " will come at once. You Karonga, will be overtaken by it before you can reach home." And so it fell out. Rain came in torrents, preceded by a great storm which overthrew a number of trees in a neighbouring estate, and greatly injured the fine avenue leading to the Mission House.

Now for some days there had been much thunder, and dark clouds covered the sky ; anyone could tell that the rain was near. But for the Konde that was just the point. The rain was there, and it was quite obviously being withheld. Why else did it not fall ? And it did fall when the wrong was righted, and the prayers offered. Who but a white man could doubt the relation of cause and effect ?

One or two local variations are worth noting. At Karonga an offering of black cloth is made along with the other things presented. In many places a pot half filled with beer is left all night at the grave where the offerings are made, and if the beer is found in the morning to have risen to the top, and filled the pot, it is a sign that the spirits have agreed to go to God with the petition. If it has not risen there is something wrong, and the wrong must be made good. It sometimes happens that the animal sacrifice is not killed, but is kept by the guardian of the grave, and belongs thenceforth, with all its issue, to the spirits. It is used just like any other cow, but it must not be sold.

An old custom seldom now followed is the children's rain dance. Boys and girls, carrying ashes in pots in one hand, and a small branch in the other, go to the cross-roads, with a leader who carries a fowl. They move with a kind of hopping and leaping dance, and, arrived at the cross-roads, they gather around the leader, who sings :

" Let all old things fly away ; we get new things from God. His house is great. He has room for everything."

Ashes and branches are now thrown in a heap, and the fowl left there, while the children return as they went, with song and dance.

It is remarkable that while rain is often so difficult to bring on, it is in the power of anyone, who has just cause, to stop it. But just cause he must have, and he must secure the co-operation of the spirits. This being done by prayer, offered by the family

representative, or by the chief if he can be induced
to do so, the person who wishes the rain to stop, ties
a bunch of feathers to his spear, dips the feathers
in red ochre, and sets the spear upright in his garden.
Or if he wishes the prohibition to act over a wide
area, the spear with the feathers is set up in some
hidden place among the reeds on the lake shore. The
rain will presently stop. One man well known to me,
takes a small piece of polished blackthorn in his hand,
and wherever he goes the rain stops. His own faith
in his powers, and the faith of many others, is quite
beyond dispute. There is an old man not far from
me whose family has possessed for many generations
the power of causing the wind to blow, or to cease
blowing, at will. The old man I speak of is believed
to have exercised his powers quite successfully in
1923.

A very few Europeans are believed to possess power
over the rain. In 1908 a house was being built at the
Overtoun Institution, Livingstonia, the residence of
the Scottish missionary, the Rev. Robert Laws,
C.M.G. The house was still unfinished when the
rains were due, and no rain fell. At last, some time
in January, the roofing was finished, and next day
rain fell in torrents. Dr. Laws had removed the
embargo! Similar powers are ascribed to another
well-known missionary, the Rev. Dr. Elmslie of
Angoniland. And still, if the rain is too much or too
little, the people say, " Ah! it is the Great One at
Livingstonia. Why is he doing this ? "

Prayer for rain is offered in one place or another

practically every year ; but it is now done in secret, an idea having got abroad that the white man disapproves of such practices. Do forbidden acts still find a place in these ceremonies ? Who can tell ? In some matters the native is as secret as the grave and the European who claims to know " all about it " is a deluded man.

CHAPTER XVII

The Foretellers

AMONG primitive peoples all over the world, the power of certain individuals to foretell events, to anticipate the future, is profoundly believed in. Western science has so organized life that such methods of meeting the future are needless and foolish. Smallpox is met at a distance, as are many other diseases, by quarantine regulations, by isolation, by skilful treatment when it comes. Hunger is warded off by foresight, by careful distribution, by skilful farming. The terror of heavenly bodies visiting our skies is neutralized by the calculations of astronomers published long beforehand.

The Konde have their own way of meeting these emergencies. Smallpox is warded off in dreams by the prophets. Hunger, in not a few cases, is anticipated by prophetic warning that rain will not fall at the usual time, and therefore food stocks must be carefully guarded. Eclipses, and even earthquakes, are foretold, not by the scientific methods of the West, but by the foretellers, whose information is as confidently trusted by the Konde, as are the calculations of science in more advanced lands.

It cannot be asserted that Konde prophecy contains much that is dramatic. It is true that those who were doomed to die in battle were known beforehand to the chief and one or two others; but such dramatic events as the bloody spectre foretelling death at Ticonderoga, at the time an unknown place; or the visions of Highland seers in Scotland; or the no less dramatic forecasts of some Hindu priests, are not to be found here. Konde prophecy, if one may give it that name, was more of an everyday affair, not so much concerned with the fate of individuals, as with the general welfare.

There are two classes of foretellers. First are the persons already referred to as *abakunguluka*. Their initiation into office has already been described, and it is enough to say that the medicines taken, and the ceremonies undergone, at the time of their installation as subordinate chiefs, gives them power to see in dreams all danger to the chief or the community. The verb *kukunguluka* means to go, or fall, down; to sink deep; and the *unkunguluka* is the man who goes down, in dreams, to the underworld, to obtain there the word that he is to deliver to the chief. *Kusololoka*, with its noun *unsololi*, has the same meaning.

The primary duty of these men was to guard the person of the chief from unseen dangers. Anything that threatened was seen in dreams, and measures taken to ward it off. Witchcraft, illness, poison, danger from animals, from falling trees, were thus foreseen. But in order effectively to protect him, they must know where he is, and what he is doing at a given time. The young chief, Reuben, the account of whose installation is given in the chapter on the chieftainship, told me that on his return home his prophets would tell him that he had been talking with me, and would demand an account of all that passed between us. These men, it may be here noted, would not give me any information about themselves or their methods; that was *mwiko* (forbidden); but they had no objection at all to the chief telling me all I wished to know. Practically all that is here said about them, therefore, is derived from various chiefs, and whatever is not so derived is common knowledge, which anyone may pick up.

When the message came to a prophet, he went to tell his fellow-prophets, and all together went to the chief, to whom all such dreams must be related, before publication to the common people, and the steps decided upon which are to be taken to ward off whatever danger threatens. War was seen, down to its smallest details. The dreamer was actually, in dreams, present at the fight, and saw both the killed and the wounded. The names were given to the chief, who, when he marched out with his forces, left behind any of these whom he wished to save. The people very confidently affirm that just the persons named, and no others, were killed. The incredulity of the white man is regarded as an entirely uncalled for slight upon upright men discharging a duty about which, to the Konde, there is no mystery at all.

The German defeat at Karonga in September, 1914, was very clearly foretold by Njuli and Mwandisi, both still living near the lake shore ; but the Germans knew nothing of the prophecy. The effect of it, however, was that no local carriers could be recruited, and most of the carriers employed were found among the Basango to the north. Next, it was asserted that the Germans would evacuate Neu Langenburg without fighting, which is what actually happened ; and, finally, about the same time, it was declared that the " first-comers " would become lords of the country. These first-comers were Mr. Moir of Glasgow and his companions, who hunted elephant north of the Songwe River in the early eighties. Dr. Laws of Livingstonia visited the north end of the lake much earlier, but that visit did not make the same impression as the more prolonged stay of Mr. Moir and his fellow-hunters.

Smallpox is the most dreaded scourge in the district. It is believed to come from the south, pass through the land, and finally to disappear among the Basango to the north, to whom the Konde consigned, with much gusto, all the evils that they were threatened or afflicted with. Its coming was foretold by the prophets, who declared that it was an act of God in punishment of wickedness. But smallpox was sometimes brought by the sorcerers. These enemies of society were caught in the act—in dreams—by the prophets, who also, in dreams, went out to meet and repel them. If the evil-doers were caught and beaten, their bodies next day would betray them, for the dream-fight is a stern reality, and the body bears the marks of battle. If the prophets succeeded in driving out all the sorcerers, no one would die of smallpox, but one remaining sorcerer could work unlimited mischief so long as he remained undiscovered.

In a community which practises "subsistence agriculture," it is important to know beforehand when the rains will be late, and it is the duty of the prophets to let the chief know, and through him the people, when this will happen. In such a contingency, the chief issues instructions, varying in minuteness, regulating the kinds of food which are to be used, and warning against greed. Punishment used to follow disregard of the prohibition, but the chiefs, although they still issue orders as before, do not now venture to punish offenders, or at any rate they punish none who would be likely to report them to the Administration.

Famine, however, was not always the result of drought. It was often, in the past, the result of war. When a powerful enemy approached, the people left the villages and took refuge in the bush, sometimes for long periods, leaving all that they could not carry to fall into the hands of the invader. The last occasion on which such a famine was foretold was when the Angoni passed through the land seeking a habitation. The people fled before them, and a famine resulted which is still traditionally remembered. With such a powerful enemy approaching, the prophets had an easy task in foreseeing famine.

The death of chiefs is also foretold. The prophets see in dreams the house of a chief being built in the spirit-world, and they know that when it is finished the person for whom it is intended must very soon go and occupy it. This vision is not told to the chief, but to those who have the duty of choosing his successor, who quietly make their arrangements while the living chief is still among them. He himself has forewarnings also, for he sees his ancestors beckoning him, and knows that his hour is near. Common people die in the common way.

No prophecies are more interesting than those which concern the European. They are found over a wide area in Bantuland, and among the Konde they were very detailed and definite. Many versions of these prophecies are still current, the most detailed being that ascribed to Mwakipesire of Masoko. With a great multitude of people the prophet climbed a small hill near Masoko, and there delivered his message.

"A man will come from the lake, white in body, and he will be lord of the whole country. War he will bring to an end, the Angoni he will conquer, the Arab he will expel. He will bring us cloth, and we shall throw away our garments of leaves. Our way of worship will come to an end, for he will tell us how to go direct to God Himself; but he will not come until all who are here to-day have gone to the spirits."

Maseke of Karonga added that the white man would come in a canoe that sent out smoke, that the peace would be so great that none would carry a spear, and that the land would be filled with wonders of which no man had ever heard.

How far the original form of these prophecies has been modified by experience, I do not undertake to say. All who pretend to knowledge of the subject vigorously deny any modification. Whether the actual performances of the white man have satisfied the expectations aroused by the prophecies, is a question susceptible of more than one answer. The great mass of the people would certainly not rejoice at the departure of the Europeans ; nevertheless there are some who would be glad to see the last of them. Long before the Great War, prophecies were freely circulating among the people, that the Germans would go away, and be succeeded by white men of another land. Just now similar prophecies are being made about the British, who are to be succeeded by another white race as yet unknown. The fact, which is well known to many people, that some " doctors " are seeking for a medicine which will cause the white man to disappear, is significant.

There is a tradition that a series of forecasts was made long ago : the Great War, the influenza which followed it, the great earthquake of 1919, and finally a great darkness which is still to come.

The progress of Christianity has not destroyed the faith, especially of the heathen, in the local prophets ; and it is not improbable that Christians still retain a conviction that these men were not wholly without Divine guidance. The chief Swebe, when I asked him whether in all cases smallpox foretold had actually come, answered with an emphatic affirmative, and with an intonation which clearly meant, " Why should it be doubted ? " The spirits form a link between men and God, and there is, in the native mind, no reason at all to doubt that God can make the future known to certain individuals when it is His will to do so. The darkness of mind, so often attributed to the heathen, is not absolute, and they themselves, while readily acknowledging the superiority of Christianity, do not admit that they were wholly without guidance in the past.

The second class of foretellers are the *abakomwa malago*, a phrase which may be roughly translated as spirit-possessed persons, trance-seers, inspired persons. They foretell the future by means of an indwelling spirit, but the occupation is always temporary. The possessed person runs about calling, " Listen, listen, listen." His friends seek to restore him by pouring water on his head, but if he resists they let him alone, believing that he has a message. He breaks away, followed by his friends, who carefully note all he says. One man known to me climbed, in that condition, a mountain of two thousand feet, and on recovering consciousness was in an exhausted condition, though he showed no signs of exhaustion while in the trance.

These seers, if we may use a short name for them, announce very much the same things as the prophets, but they seem to have made the forecasting of animal visitations their special province. In 1920 a woman called Nakanjere declared that a lion would come and kill many people. The chief, Mwenemusuku, protected his land in the manner described in the chapter on " The Powers of Evil," and none of his people were killed, though the total killed by a lion in that year in neighbouring districts was very large. A letter in my possession puts the number at forty, while others say fifty. Where the chief protected his land in the traditional way, the people were safe ; where this was not done, the toll of human lives was great.

In 1922 the same woman predicted that, for the sins of the people, a spotted hyena would kill many. Again the chief protected his land, and again no one was killed ; while in a neighbouring and unprotected land, the death-roll was considerable. In the same year leopards were predicted in the Nserya district. The chief was urged to sacrifice an ox, but refused. Six people were killed, and a number of mauled men and women were treated by Dr. Brown at the Mission at Itete.

To the Konde, as I have already said, there is no difficulty in connecting prediction and fulfilment. The inspiration of the foretellers is not doubted ; the animals came as foretold ; why should reasonable men refuse to acknowledge a relation between the two events ? At any rate it may be presumed that the native will go on seeing a connection, while the white man will fall back upon the ever-ready doctrine of coincidence, and refuse upon any terms to acknowledge any other relation.

There is, however, spirit possession of another kind,

which is still a terror to many people : sheer evil spirits, who seek to take possession of a human being as a dwelling-place. Possessed children hide themselves, crying out, "*Abandu, abandu*" (men, men). Adults reveal their possession by dashing about, dancing, shouting. If the possessed makes for water, it is known that a water spirit has entered into him ; if he goes to the hills, it is a mountain spirit. In either case the patient is taken by the medicine man to a waterfall, "where God dwells," and given medicine to drink. If he resists, force is used, but frequently the doctor is impressive enough to succeed without it. A bell is rung ; the doctor speaks, " We have found you. Come out of the man." Then he takes water into his mouth and squirts it on the breast and back of the afflicted person, striking him at the same time with the calabash from which he took the water, and holding it for a little over the patient's head. Next he sprinkles the whole body with flour, and the party returns to the village, where every one is required to drink a medicine administered by the doctor ; for when the spirit goes out of its present victim, he will seek another dwelling, but the medicine protects all who drink it from invasion. The patient must not shave his head for six to eight months, nor may he eat flesh of any kind. When the period prescribed is over, the doctor comes to shave the head of the patient, who has now recovered, and eats part of a fowl which has been treated with yet another medicine.

CHAPTER XVIII

Divination & the Lot

THE fact of death is not regarded by the tribes of Central Africa as forming a barrier between the living and the dead. The two form one community, and the means of communication between them are naturally therefore well developed. Living and dead are mutually dependent, and a certain amount of goodwill must necessarily exist between them. What the dead cannot do for themselves, the living must do for them ; and what the living must know, but do not, the dead can tell them if properly interrogated. It is upon this fact that divination depends, as do omens also to some extent. The use of charms and amulets, however, depends upon the other, and perhaps closely related fact, that Nature is not a fixed system of laws pursuing its way regardless of human needs, but is pliable, responsive, and will advise, protect, injure, according to the means used by those who possess the power.

The idea that the whole system of consultation of the spirits, of the interpretation of omens, and of the use of charms and amulets, is based upon conscious deception—a few clever men in each community taking advantage of the credulity of the masses—can be entertained only by those who have acquired no insight into the native mind and its working. It is impossible to maintain that a system, as wide as a continent, and as persistent as the centuries, should be the outcome of an age-long conspiracy to cheat. The human mind does not work in that way. The system is involved in the world-view; it is woven into the mind-texture of the people, and the honesty of the " practitioners " is, in many cases, as indubitable as the faith of the people.

The prayer for rain, for instance, is offered with a simple sincerity, as honest as any petition ever offered in a Christian church. I am not asserting that the prayer brings the rain; nor yet that it does not. Nor do I suppose that the diviner is in touch with fact, when he uses what he considers to be means of getting into communication with the spirits. I am arguing only for the honesty, in a great majority of cases, of the men who do these things. They are men with a conviction.

The diviner usually hands on his knowledge and his office to one of his own family; but an outsider may learn his secrets by paying an ox or a cow. I am not aware that there is any serious attempt to guard the secrets of the profession, though the various drugs used are not made known except to those who are willing to pay the fee. The only form of initiation is the incising of medicines into the arms or wrists of the initiate, and this incision may be renewed should occasion require it.

Divining is resorted to primarily in cases of illness :
to find the cause and suggest the cure. But it is used
on many other occasions; indeed almost anything that
one wants to know, he may bring to the diviner. One
may require information about lost or stolen goods ;
another may want to know whether a thieving expedi-
tion will be successful ; and the diviner's art is at the
service of both. Success in hunting or fishing may be
inquired about ; news of absent friends may be had ;
the reason why the gardens yield a poor crop ; will
the inquirer get work from the European to whom he
purposes applying, and will the pay be good ? These
and numerous other matters are brought for answer
to the diviner.

In 1922 the store of an unusually intelligent native
trader was burned down, and cash to the amount of
£170 was stolen. The trader went to a diviner, and
paid him a fee of five pounds, in return for which
he was informed that after a certain time had passed
his money would all be restored. About the middle
of October, 1923, the whole had been paid in, but
whether the date corresponded with the time given
by the diviner, I do not know ; and it should be added
that the local magistrate at Karonga took up the case
with great vigour, a fact which no doubt had its effect.

I was present in 1902 at an act of divination of which
I was myself the subject. During the course of a
long journey I had entered a village with only two
men, all the other carriers having fallen behind. The
villagers took me for an " undesirable," and refused
the usual salutations ; but when my men arrived,

they realized that an error had been committed. The diviner was called to find out whether I would wish to wipe out the insult, and I had the opportunity of seeing the process. The diviner, a middle-aged man, sat on the ground with a flat stone in front of him, and in his hand a short stick about six inches long, which he grasped in the middle, while the top was held by a lanky youth, evidently anyone chosen at random for the purpose. The diviner moved the stick up and down, striking it sometimes on the stone, sometimes on the ground to right or left of the stone, repeating at the same time words of which all I understood were the word for " God," and that for " white man." I smiled at the performance, and in a little the diviner declared that the spirits refused to speak, a result which, as I afterwards learned, was due to my incredulous smiles. The same afternoon he and I went out together to hunt ; he with bow and arrows, I with a modern rifle ; and the same ill-success attended the efforts of both.

The methods of divining are many, and only a few of them can be given here. The general outline, however, is the same, or nearly so, in all cases. Eliminating questions are asked, gradually limiting the range of possibility, until the correct answer has been found. Is the sick man going to die ? If not, what is the disease due to ? God ? A spirit ? Who ? His father ? Elder brother ? etc. etc. What is the disease ? Is it this, or that, or the other ? What does the offended spirit want ? a cow, sheep, goat ? and is it to be killed or not ? One illustration must suffice. The father of a sick child went a few months ago to a diviner, who told him that the illness was due to his own folly in not sacrificing a cow at the funeral of his father, who had died recently. " Go and pray," said the diviner, " I will give you no medicine." After prayer, a cow was killed, and due observance made of the ritual demanded, after which the child recovered. If the sickness is due to the anger of a living person, who has persuaded his ancestors to avenge him for some wrong done, the diviner directs that an appropriate offering be brought to the offended man, who thereupon requests the spirits to remove their anger, and the patient recovers.

A few of the methods may now be briefly described.

I. *Ikipiki*, the stick, or cup. A hollowed-out, cup-shaped piece of wood, perhaps three inches long, is moved backwards and forwards over a piece of banana stalk, the open end of the cup downwards, and questions are asked as described. When the cup refuses to move, the right question has been asked, and the answer thereby given. In the act of divination that I saw here a few months ago, the diviner seemed honestly unable to move the cup, though in my own hand it moved easily.

II. *Isiba*. The horn of a small buck is filled with medicines, and placed with its base on the ground. When questions are asked, it begins to sway, and stands still again when the right question has been put.

III. *Isyabwe* is a recent importation from another district. The diviner, having drunk a medicine called *musika*, sits on the dark side of the door, having in his hand a small calabash partly filled with sand; the inquirer sits on the other side of the door. The diviner shakes his calabash, saying, "Speak, Mulambya, who dwellest by the clear waters ; tell me what disease this man is suffering from." He soon begins to feel a rising in the throat, which causes him to speak in a falsetto voice, "*He, tata.*" The falsetto now gives way to the natural voice, in which the questions are put, the answer, coming in falsetto, being the response of the spirit. It would be interesting to know whether the *musika* medicine has qualities which cause the throat to contract so as to produce a falsetto voice, but the point is one upon which I have no information.

IV. *Wa m'maboko*, the hands. When an inquirer chooses this method, the diviner goes to the bush, whence he takes a *kilago*, a rush-like grass about eighteen inches in length. Detaching the rootlets, he chews them carefully, and spits the juice into his hands. The palms being rubbed smoothly over each other, the questions are put, and when the hands stick, the answer has been given.

V. *Kayamba*, the tortoise. The intestines of the tortoise are removed, and a cord passed through the mouth and the anus. The cord is held upright by the left hand, while the tortoise is lifted with the right as each question is put. When the right question is asked, the tortoise, instead of falling to the ground, stops half-way on the string. This form of divination is very widely known among the tribes around Lake Nyasa.

VI. *Indeko*, the pot. An axe-head is fixed upright
in the ground, and a pot containing water and medicine is balanced on the edge. If the pot falls and
breaks, the patient will not recover; if it keeps its
balanced position, he will soon be well. The diviner
Mwankosore, who showed me this method, added
that in the case of an illness discovered by this method
to be due to witchcraft, he gave his walking-stick to
the patient, who immediately got up and walked,
perfectly whole. I shall have occasion again to refer
to recoveries of this nature.

When the diviner is consulted with regard to theft,
a different procedure is followed.

I. *Ikifwani*, the image. This savours more of
magic than of divining, but it is placed here because
it is called by the latter name by those who practise
it. An incident which took place in 1918 will make
the method clear. In that year there was scarcity of
food, and consequent theft from gardens and store-
houses. One man went to the diviner, and asked him
to find the goods and the thief. The diviner took a
small image of a man, about two feet in height, made
from a block of wood. In the head was a cavity, into
which medicine was put, and the cavity closed. The
party went to the garden from which the food had
been stolen, and, the image being laid on the ground,
the diviner prayed to it to lead them to the thief. It
was then taken up in the right hand of a strong man,
and presently began to shake violently, so that it could
with difficulty be held. In a little it swayed in one
direction, and the holder moved thither, the whole

party following, until the shaking of the image ceased in a garden. Digging at that spot, the stolen food was discovered ; and the image, being asked now to find the thief, led them to a certain house, the owner of which at once confessed the theft, and paid a cow as fine. A similar incident occurred in 1919, when a number of hoes were stolen. The person accused by the image vigorously denied guilt, but gave in when threatened with the poison test, and paid a cow as fine. In this case the confession, as indeed in both cases, may have been due to fear of what would happen in the poison ordeal, and the fine paid rather than undergo further trials, even although the accused persons were not really guilty.

II. *Ulupembe*, the horn. Recently a cow was stolen, and the owner went to a diviner for help, taking with him a piece of the halter by which the cow had been tethered in the house. The diviner made a fire by rubbing two sticks together, and as the smoke ascended, he added to the smouldering fire tiny bits of the rope, along with some of his own medicines, and as the smoke increased, the diviner directed it to go towards the village where the thief lived. Noting the direction in which the smoke moved, he told the owner to wait until some one died in that village, at the same time bidding him on no account weep for the dead man, for then the medicine would kill him also. If the bladder of the first person to die showed signs of blackness, there need be no doubt that he was the thief, and his friends would be obliged to pay over a cow. For the nearest relative of the dead man would go to the diviner to find out the cause of the discoloration, and would of necessity make reparation.

III. A few years ago a policeman had his goods stolen at Mwaya. Instead of reporting to the proper quarters, he went to a diviner, who sprinkled the policeman's house with medicine, which he publicly declared would kill the thief, and in a short time the goods were brought to the chief of the district. The deception in this case is too obvious to call for comment.

Inquiries regarding hunting and fishing, and every other kind of question, are conducted in ways similar to those already given. Employment with a white man is evidently still a matter for careful consideration, and it is entirely possible that the diviner prevents many a man from going to work who would otherwise be glad to go. "Shall I find work?" "Shall I find peace?" "Shall I get good wages?" The second question is much the most important, and means, "Shall I be employed by a white man who is not a perpetual scold?" the kind of European whom the native hates and fears more than anything else.

The fee paid to the diviner varied from about a halfpenny to an ox or a cow.

While there is undoubtedly deliberate cheating and charlatanry, these should be regarded, not as the essence of the system, but its excrescence. In many cases, if not in all, the diviner has subconsciously decided what answer shall be given ; in the region of the subconscious his mind is made up, and, there being no opposing idea, the " mental process issues in a conation which passes over into the physical motor response " (Tansley). The image in the mind, of the divining rod acting in the manner conceived, tends to become a physical fact, and the rod comes to a halt in obedience to a previously formed decision, of which the operator is, in most cases, not consciously aware. Nevertheless the opportunities for deception are many.

Ifipendo, the lot. The lot is resorted to in a variety of cases, but its application is much more limited than that of divination.

I. When divination has decided that an illness is due to poison, the lot is invoked to find the poisoner. Little pieces of dough are kneaded into as many tiny cups as there are persons suspected. Into each is put a small quantity of *mwafi* (the poison used for the ordeal), and the suspected persons are then invited to take each the cup that he selects for himself, the preparations having been made, of course, in their absence. The guilty person is he who takes the cup in which the poison remains unabsorbed into the dough, the others being assumed to have vomited. This might just as well be called a way of undergoing the poison ordeal, but as it is called *ifipendo* it is included here.

II. In cases of disputed inheritance no poison is put into the cups, but a little dry flour. The claimant who selects the cup in which the moisture from the dough has penetrated to the dry flour is declared to be the rightful heir.

When the rain stops, and no natural cause can be assigned, it is assumed to be the act of some person unknown. Now when a common man stops the rain, he must first have obtained the assistance of his chief ; and the chief, being discovered by the method just described, must take measures to have the evil undone.

III. If a question arises as to the ownership of some article, small sticks are set upright in the ground. The claimants sit each opposite his own stick, and he whose stick first falls, if it falls towards him, is the rightful owner. But if the stick falls towards another person, then that person is declared the owner. Finally, if goods of any kind are divided into lots, one lot for each of a number of persons, sticks are taken, marked to correspond with the lots. Each shareholder picks out a stick, the marks, of course, not being shown to him, and gets the goods which correspond to the marks. There is no appeal, the decision of the lot is final.

The poison ordeal, though now prohibited, and administered only in secret, was, until European government began to put it down, so common that a description of it comes in appropriately in any chapter dealing with native life ; and as it has been referred to here already, the method of administering to individuals will be given now, leaving administration to a whole community for the chapter on "Witchcraft." The ordeal was applied for reasons grave or trivial, from an accusation of murder down to a petty family quarrel of no importance except in a moment of ill-temper. Both parties to a quarrel or an accusation went to the doctor, and stated their case. He took a piece of bark of the *mwafi* tree for each, raised it a little in his hand and let it fall to the ground ; if one turned round in falling and the other fell without turning, the doctor knew beforehand which was the guilty person—he whose bark turned round in falling. The poison was then prepared from the bark by the doctor, by whom it was administered next day. The one who vomited was in the right, the other in the wrong.

Assuming that the poison was honestly administered, that is to say, that the doctor did not give a strong mixture to one and a weak to another, which he very probably did in many cases, must it be assumed that the result was merely fortuitous ? Is it not a psychological possibility that the consciousness of guilt in the one case, and of innocence in another, causes the poison in the stomach to act in the way that generations of belief in its efficacy has led the whole community to expect that it would act ? I do not suggest that this happened in all cases. No doubt the generations have seen countless cases of tragic miscarriage of justice ; on the other hand, so many confessions have followed conviction under the ordeal, that it is difficult to believe that in all cases the discovery of the guilty person was a mere fortuity.

CHAPTER XIX

Omens & Portents

TO us the universe is continually offering the gift of knowledge. The earth and the starry heavens, all that goes on in the human mind, and all men's actions, are subjects of inquiry. But our gift has to be received with toil of heart and brain, for it is granted only to men of mental vigour.

To the Konde, on the other hand, what the universe offers is not so much knowledge as foreknowledge; information rather than education. Prescience, perhaps because the Konde is so distrustful of his own unaided powers, is more to him than the heaped-up lore of the centuries. Everything is in the hands of unseen powers, and it is important for weak men to know beforehand what is the attitude of these powers to any undertaking he may have in mind.

Nature is not, to the African, a fixed system of laws that cannot be interfered with; men can and do interfere with it; stop the rain, injure the crops, make serpents, call up lions and leopards, and many other things. Now it might almost *a priori* be asserted that such a system will not stop at being controllable: it will also be predictive, it will give signs and tokens of what is coming. But these signs and tokens are not the act of an impersonal universe ; they are the act of God, a revelation of His care for men.

In Konde omens and portents the dramatic element is slight. I can retail nothing to equal in creepiness the cry of the Irish banshee, or Highland dogs barking at an invisible funeral, or the family ghost clanking its chain in an old English mansion. But a Konde dog howls at night, and sudden silence falls upon the previously laughing and chatting company sitting around the fire, or out in the cool moonlight. Who is going to die ? And when ? And of what sickness ? Or a branch creaks in the forest as one is passing through it at night ; and the belated traveller hastens his steps without looking backward, for that way lies death. The bold man who passes the grave of a chief at night, and hears his name called, takes to his heels, eyes front for his very life, for the backward look is death, though to the closed eye there is little danger that cannot be averted.

Omens are offered by nature ; they come spontaneously, so far as men are concerned. There are cases in which the omens are consulted, or taken, but generally the information is given by events, rather than discovered by experiment, as with the ancient Roman augurs. And although some men know more about them than others, there are no specialists to whom a fee has to be paid for the interpretation of the omen.

The rough classification which is here attempted, makes no pretence of being exhaustive. Life is full of hints and tokens of the goodwill or illwill of the unseen powers, and the wise man is he who profits by them where that is possible ; where it is not possible, he is the wise man who quietly awaits the event, thankful that at least the misfortune does not take him at unawares, and that, if he cannot ward off the danger, he can meet it with an equanimity impossible to one upon whom the blow falls suddenly.

1. Weather lore is strangely absent, perhaps because in the tropics there is a regularity about the weather which renders prognostication as unnecessary as barometers. If, on a rainy evening, the crow caws on a high note, it will be hot the next day, with a cloudless sky ; if on a low note the rain will continue. Another token of rain is given when the long-necked, long-legged birds, *mwankusye*, fly in a line abreast towards the lake.

2. Of bad news there are countless indications ; of good news only a very few hints have come to light. Twitching of the upper eyelid indicates good fortune of some kind undefined ; but if the twitching is in the lower lid, death is near, of the person whose eye twitches, or of a friend.

3. Before the settlement of the country by the Europeans, long journeys were rarely undertaken, and omens on the way were carefully watched for, and as carefully heeded when they were given. Serpents are the most trusted mediums and great significance is attached to their movements. A serpent lying on one side of the path, and slipping into the bush on that side as the travellers approach, indicates a clear

path. But if the serpent crosses to the other side and into the bush, the way is closed, and the travellers will return to their homes, no matter how near their destination they may be. What will happen if they continue their journey is not clear ; some undefined evil will overtake them. Parties on the war-path heeded this warning, for it was an omen of defeat if they went on, which, naturally, they never did. If the snake escapes into a hole, it indicates a death at the nearest village ; and if a python is seen on the road, the travellers, whose path is not closed, may expect to find the death-wail going on at the first village they come to.

A two-headed snake, whatever that may be, is a sure sign of death at the place one is going to ; and two snakes fighting indicate coming evil, which can only be averted by returning to the place whence one has set out. A tree falling across a path, is another warning, which no man disregards ; but the tree must fall within view of the person to whom the hint is given ; trees that have fallen otherwise have no significance. But it is worth noting that natives travelling with white men pay no heed to any omens. They are protected by the power of the European, and any significance the omens may have is his affair.

4. Travellers have their tokens on the way : the people to whom they go have foretokens of their approach. If the fire " speaks," if it makes a burring noise in the flame ; if the hens go about uttering low cries ; if *amayogobera*, small black birds with white

DANCING AT A FEAST.

The dance includes striking contortions, supported in the air, as this woman is.   Boys
standing on the ground will bend backward until their heads come near their thighs.
Walking on the hands, throwing a somersault, doing a catherine wheel are all in the
native mind dancing, and may be indulged in at any moment, as it occurs to the dancer.

breasts, sit on a tree near the house; if *mwanjala*, little black and white birds of another species, hop about twittering; the approach of strangers is foretold. Hospitality to strangers is a primary virtue among the Konde, and food is prepared at once; but it is not cooked until they actually arrive. To offer them food already cooked, is to offer a cold welcome, and possibly to do an injury; for cold food must not be eaten by chiefs, nor by hunters, nor by doctors, for in all these cases the effect would be to destroy the power of the medicines by virtue of which they are assured of success in their various callings.

5. Omens having reference to food are numerous, and a few examples must suffice. If a fly goes into one's mouth, it is a sure sign that the person will soon be eating flesh, a rare treat for the Konde, who seldom eat flesh, unless there is an occasion for it : a birth, a marriage, or a death. But the fly indicates none of these; the flesh hinted at is a pure gift with no kind of condition attached. The same good fortune is suggested if a child eats cinders from the fire-place. A leopard crying all night in the neighbourhood is giving information that some one has broken a food prohibition. New season's food has been eaten before the chief has laid an offering of the first-fruits of that particular food-stuff at the grave of his ancestors, and the dwellers in the underworld are angry at the insult offered them. The chief is informed of the crying of the leopard, and the diviner is called in to find the culprit.

There is a common grass called *ditika*, which in

Q

appearance is not unlike *malesi*, from which beer is
made. If anyone eats this while there is abundance
of proper food, it is an omen of famine to come. If the
offender is a child, he is not beaten; but if he is
grown up, he is mercilessly dealt with. It is not pretended that the beating averts the evil, nor has the
man's action in eating the *ditika* anything to do with
the coming famine, except to foretell it. If one asks,
Why then is he beaten? the answer is simply that
having foretold evil he deserves to be beaten. This
unpalatableness of plain truth (if it is plain truth) is
not unknown among other races than the Bantu.

6. Elephants while being hunted impart a great
deal of varied information to the hunters. As elephant
hunting by natives has long been prohibited, the
omens afforded are no longer available, but that does
not affect the belief in them. " The elephant does
not lie " is an assured conviction in the minds of the
hunters, and when an omen was given, the hunt was
abandoned until the matter was investigated.

If, as the hunters approach, elephants are found
leaping upon each other, a halt is called; both
because in that condition they are specially dangerous,
and because the omen is otherwise bad. There is sin
among the hunters, and the whole party returns to
the *fitembe*, the temporary quarters erected for the
hunting period. There the case is gone into. Some
one has wronged his neighbour in the manner suggested by the action of the elephants, and nothing
can be done until it is put right. To go on with the
hunt would be the extremest folly, and if no one

confesses, the party returns to the village, and the diviner is called to discover the culprit.

If two elephants are found kneeling and facing each other, some one's wife has erred in his absence, and the hunt is stopped until justice is done. An elephant taking up dust with his trunk and offering it to another, shows that some one has offered snuff to another man's wife, a most significant action, demanding immediate satisfaction. If an elephant is seen touching the teats of another, a similar action has been committed in the village, and again the hunt stops for inquiry and punishment. Trumpeting elephants are a sign of quarrelling in the village, and one plastering its face with mud is a sign of death, for the women at the death-wail cover their faces with mud or chalk. The hunters return, and do not resume until all is clear again. It is most important that not only the hunters should be free from evil, but their friends also, for evil brings them into danger, and it is the duty of all in the village to see that the natural dangers of the hunt are not increased by unnatural evil in their homes.

7. War was foretold by the prophets, but confirmatory signs were usually not wanting. If the horns of the new moon were of unequal length, an enemy was known to be approaching ; necessarily an enemy from a distance, for the phenomenon must have been visible over a wide area. The same terror was announced by a cow bellowing at night, if there was no known cause for its outcry. This, naturally, is a thing of the past, as war, at least native war, has

ceased. What significance would now be attached to these omens, I do not know. The buffalo, like the elephant, does not lie, and wise men heed its warnings. Many years ago a man called Masapa went to the Kinga region, where he quarrelled with the people, and barely escaped with his life. His chief, Mwaisumo, took up the quarrel, and prepared to invade the enemy's territory, undeterred by the predictions of defeat which came in dreams to his prophets, until, on the way, one of his men was killed by a buffalo, and this was a warning not to be disregarded. On their return home, they were received by their women folks, not with contempt and mocking, but as wise men, who were too wary to tempt " Providence " by foolish action. One more war omen. If a man, on the point of leaving for the field of battle, was suddenly, but accidentally, seized by the wrist by his wife, he laid down his weapons, and quietly stayed at home ; not for him the joy of battle ; he would have been killed, and no one thought the worse of him for heeding the omen.

8. Foretokens of death are so numerous that it is difficult even to classify them. Whatever is rare, or unnatural, or sudden, may be taken as a warning of approaching death. A mole seen by day, is a rare event, and full of dread. A Christian living near me saw this wonder in February, 1923, and in the same month he got news of the death of a friend a hundred miles away ! No connection ? He thought there was. To see the *kasuchi*, a small aquatic animal, is to see something so rare that its appearance must be the

foretoken of widespread death; but no one known to me has had the misfortune to see it. Foxes are said to have increased so greatly since the advent of the white man, that no significance is now attached to their crying; but a generation ago it announced the approaching death of a great chief. There was an interesting recrudescence of this belief in 1914. In July of that year there was a great barking of foxes in the neighbourhood of the Overtoun Institution (outside the Konde country). The news spread far, and the general anticipation of widespread disaster was held to have been amply justified when the first intimation of the Great War was received. A dog howling at night, surely nothing uncommon, still predicts death, and the dog is beaten, not because its howling brings on the evil, or because the beating can avert it; it foretells misfortune, and the forecast is unwelcome, and the unfortunate retailer of information must suffer for lack of common sense.

A cock crowing at night, when no cock should crow, is a foretoken of death, and in the first place of its own; no second time would that cock be the harbinger of news so unwelcome. Sudden things, again, an unexpected collapse of a house which looks strong, or of a tree which shows no sign of decay; or of a grave which is being digged, or a pot of beer which falls without obvious cause; these are all of dreadful omen, indicating the death of a chief. The father of the present chief Kabeta, living near Rungwe, was a great planter of trees. As he lay dying, all the trees which he had planted in his youth fell one after another, and when Kabeta went to his fathers, he had no more trees to his credit than when he was born. The fall of the village tree, planted at the installation of the chief, shows that he in whose honour it was planted is about to go to the spirit-land.

9. The heavens give very few signs. If the full moon is red, with a red circle around it, plague is coming. If the sun "builds a house" (*nimbus*), some woman is about to give birth to twins. Worst of all, naturally, is an eclipse. "*Kyala asambwike*," they say, "God has lost patience, He is going to kill us all," and they go out with drums and wild shoutings to induce the Supreme Being to go away to the Basango.

What has been described in the foregoing paragraphs is called *kusura*, to foreshadow, forecast, the agent being entirely unconscious of the significance of the action. There is another class of actions which also forecast; but although the difference is not very obvious, a different word is used, *kusikura*, which sometimes means to insult, but commonly to act as a pointer to coming evil. Such actions are mostly un-natural; many of them are in themselves evil, and their occurrence is regarded as a portent.

1. Unnatural anger. Anger in a child is a pheno-menon of awe. If a grown-up person arouses it—not in his own child—that person has received warning that his death is near. How this comes about is not clear. Some natives say that the anger is a sign, which cannot be explained; others that the child

has a disease, from which he does not himself suffer, but which passes over to the person who arouses the wrath.

At Karonga, if two old men fight with their fists, and tear each other's garments, they have forecasted death for each other. The death of a friend of one or the other will shortly take place. Among the Banyakyusa to the north, the fight of any two, young or old, with fists only, is a portent of the same significance. Such anger blazes up suddenly, and the two men fly at each other in blind fury, unable to restrain themselves sufficiently to go and fetch the weapons with which reasonable men fight. The fist as a weapon of war is not highly regarded by Africans generally, however dear it may be to others.

2. Unnatural actions. To invite an old man to climb a tree may seem to us more laughable than deadly; but to the Konde it is a dreadful combination of insult and forecast; it is a forecast, because such a thing is an insult so great as to be in itself a portent. The number of things that come under this head is legion; but generally, to ask an old person to do what is unnatural for an old person to do, is *kusikura*. Little girls quite innocently removing their scanty covering in the presence of an old man, have unwittingly warned him that his days are near an end. Perhaps under the same category we may include an invitation given by a child to an old man to come and eat; to us it could not come in a more charming way; but the old Konde would turn his back indignantly on the ill-bred brat who

so insulted him. This does not apply to an invitation to drink beer, but no one can explain why there is a difference.

3. Accusations against a man of good character come under the same heading. Some evil has been done, and the wrong-doer has not been discovered. Then, perhaps in joke, or it may be out of personal dislike, some one says that so and so did it. The person referred to knows that his days will not be long in the land. " Did I ever do a thing like that ? " he asks indignantly. " Why, then, am I accused ? " It can only be *kusikura*, and he expects to die, at the best, within a year or two.

4. If the spirits, in dreams, offer food, it must not be accepted, even in the dream : to accept it means death.

Connected with the foregoing, but having a different name among the Konde, are insults or injuries to parents. A man who fights with his father, and throws him down, has achieved the final wickedness. Whether the old man was right or wrong in the matter in dispute is of no consequence ; the whole community expresses its abhorrence of the deed. " Has this man reached even to God ? " that is to say, does he consider himself the equal of God, that he does such things ? Word is sent to the chief, and the whole district is informed of the evil thing that has been done. There is no formal denunciation, no spoken curse ; but the *ikugune*, the curse of all fathers, and of all ancestors, is upon the son. He becomes lame ; then unable to stand upright ; finally he crawls about on his buttocks, a helpless object. The curse has taken effect.

After a time good-natured people try to bring father and son together again. The son is persuaded to make his father an offering of an ox or a cow in token of repentance. If the father agrees, a day is fixed, and the whole community, including the little children, assembles at the house of the injured father. Beer is prepared, the ox is killed, the son publicly expresses his repentance, and the father his acceptance thereof. Then the people, having heard all the details of the crime, express their feelings in a prolonged groan. A dose of medicine is now given to the son, a stick is put into his hands, and he is bidden to rise and walk, which he does in the presence of all! A similar curse falls upon the man who does evil with one of his father's wives; and there are a very few other crimes which automatically bring on the same punishment.

It is not difficult, from the point of view of modern mental science, to explain the facts. The disability is due to the conviction in the mind of the younger man, strengthened by a similar conviction in the mind of the whole community, that such results always follow deeds like his. Similar phenomena are by no means unknown among Europeans, where the response to each other of mind and body is not so immediate as it is among the more unsophisticated Konde. The man bearing his sin is mentally, perhaps, rather than physically, unable to stand upright; and the conviction having been removed from his mind, the disability naturally leaves his body. Relax the conviction, and the disease will be relaxed; destroy it, and the disease will vanish, having no objective reality.

But how do the people regard the whole event? What has caused the disability, and what has removed it? There can be no doubt as to the answer. Sin and its consequences in the one case; reconciliation and consequent removal of the penalty in the other. This explanation, though held by native Christians, is also held by the heathen; and in any case it is not the teaching of Christianity to-day that diseases due to sin are removed immediately reconciliation between God and man has taken place, so that even a knowledge of Christian doctrine would not explain the presence of the conviction in the native mind. The idea, if not the form of words, is found, at least in germ, in every act of propitiation offered to offended spirits; the appropriate offering having been made, and reconciliation effected, the penalty passes away.

CHAPTER XX

The Powers of Evil: I. Witchcraft

BELIEF in witchcraft is not among the things that are passing away. So universal is the belief in its malign powers that anyone, except a Christian, who dares to express doubts on the matter, is himself in danger of being denounced as a practiser of the black art. It fills the whole outlook of the common people. If one is persistently ill, and medicines do not cure him, he suspects some one of practising against him ; if children die one after the other, both parents cannot escape suspicion, one or other is guilty ; if cattle do not give a normal quantity of milk, some one has bewitched them. And there is not a house in all heathen Konde-land that is not, in one way or another, or in many ways, protected by charms and medicines against the power of witchcraft.

Witchcraft in Europe is a power gained by traffic with the Evil One, and used by the possessor either for his or her own ends, or hired out for payment. Now among the Konde an *undosi*, witch or wizard, is as much the creation of God as other men are. "God has made men in many images," and upon a few He has bestowed those mysterious and evil powers in the presence of which common men, if unprotected, are so helpless.

While common men dread nothing so much as an accusation of witchcraft, there are swaggering fellows, great doctors and others, who boast openly of their powers; and so great is the dread in which they are held, that no one dares to cross them, or to have them brought to trial. All chiefs of any standing are credited with the power of witchcraft, but in their case it is supposed to be a special endowment to enable them to maintain their position against evil-doers.

Witchcraft is hereditary; men and women are born with it; born with two *isota*, serpents, in the stomach, by the power of which they can leave the body, and go about at night, unseen, to work their evil will on man and beast. If a parent is *undosi*, the children will be also; but if an expectant mother knows that her husband is a wizard, she will take care to have her child born at a distance, so that it cannot inherit its father's undesirable powers. If inherited from the mother, it is of peculiar virulence; but if from the father, the powers sometimes lie quiescent, and do no harm to anyone. If the *post mortem* reveals tokens of witchcraft on the left side, it has come from the mother; if on the right, from the father.

The Konde recognize three degrees of power, or of wickedness, in witchcraft. There are the comparatively harmless persons who drink the milk of cows at night, but do no other harm; their punishment, if discovered, is to herd the cattle the whole of the next day ; next, those who destroy men and cattle, and everything else, by means of their hidden powers ; and finally, the creators of lions, leopards, crocodiles, and eagles, who are the worst enemies of society, but who are held in such fear that they are seldom molested. The official dreamers, already frequently referred to, have one *isota*, serpent, in the stomach, but they are not called wizards ; they are witch destroyers, or at least discoverers, for they have the power of seeing in dreams what these evil men are doing, and in dreams going out to fight them. And if, in the dream, the dreamer kills the snake with which he fights, the owner will be found dead in the morning.

Perhaps one of the commonest charges of witch-craft is made in connection with the milk supply. As a rule, in December, the chief sends out word that he expects the milk supply to be good for the year ; if it turns out to be less than was expected, and if there has been no drought, it is obvious that there has been undue interference, and that on a great scale, with the cattle. The whole of the people of the affected district are summoned to the chief's village, and put to the test ; each person bringing all the cattle he possesses. There are two tests : by the ear, and by the stomach, that is to say by poison. The people sit in a great circle, and one after another comes up to the doctor, who bores the ear with a sharp instru-ment ; if the ear is easily bored, the person is inno-cent : if the skin is tough, and resists, he is guilty, and is ordered to sit on one side, where he is joined by all others who are found out in the same way.

But each person who is declared innocent goes at once, without further parley, to take charge of the cattle which he brought to the meeting. From the guilty persons everything is taken away : cattle, hoes, cooking pots, food stocks ; and men are sent at once to burn down their houses. The live stock is the property of the chief, and it is mostly killed on the spot, and eaten, or dried, before the assembly departs ; while the wretched criminals are sent out into the world, homeless and in poverty. They are not always expelled from the district, but they usually prefer to go to another chief.

The poison test has the same results for the guilty ; but every individual is not necessarily tested. From each village one man is taken, and he drinks for the whole of that community. If he vomits, not only he, but all the village which he represents is innocent. If he does not, it does not follow that he is himself the guilty person, but only that the criminal (or criminals) will be found in his village. They are taken individually, and the poison administered, the innocent vomiting, and the guilty failing to do so. The decoction is never strong enough among the Konde to kill, and therefore other punishments must be found. Not infrequently a dog or a cock is made to take the poison, the results being credited or debited to the person for whom it stands.

The " smelling out " of witches is not generally practised ; but there is a woman at Tukuyu, a stout young woman with a hearty laugh, who has the power of picking out the innocent when a general accusation of witchcraft is made. The people are assembled by order of the chief, and the woman walks slowly round the circle, gazing into the eyes of each person, and eliminating the innocent one by one, using no other test than the look in the individual's eyes. Those who remain are guilty.

Prosperity in another arouses all the evil passions of witches and wizards. But prosperity in itself was, until lately, evidence that the prosperous person was himself a wizard. There is a woman living not far from me who was accused before the British magistrate of pretending to exercise witchcraft, and to obtain cattle and other goods by threatening violence. She was dismissed on technical grounds, but ordered not to return to her own district. In conversation with her after the trial she told me that it was only the presence of the white man that saved her from being burned alive as a witch; the evidence against her being the rapid increase of her live stock. But the increase, she assured me, was " the gift of God."

Death by burning was the ancient penalty when that was inflicted publicly; but when the witches or wizards themselves undertook to kill a fellow-sorcerer in jealousy, they did it in another way. Leaving their bodies behind them, they go to the house of the victim, enter by the roof, disturbing nothing; and finally enter the stomach of the sleeping person. Thence they wander about to lungs, heart, or liver, and wound him with their " secret spears." Next day the man is ill, and the day following he dies. If the *post mortem* reveals ulcers on heart, lungs, or liver, it is entirely satisfactory evidence that death was due to witchcraft. The whole population is called up, and the chief directs the application of the poison test, in the manner already described. If the culprits are not discovered, they bring the body of the victim to the surface without disturbing the soil (an art the secret of which is now confined to a very few persons), and indulge in a ghoulish cannibal feast. At Karonga in 1913 a suspicion arose that this had happened, and men who had enjoyed the benefits of many years' training at the Overtoun Institution told me that they did not believe that such things happened now, since Christ had destroyed the powers of evil, but they had no doubt whatever that they happened frequently in the past.

Smallpox is popularly supposed to be due, in many cases, to witchcraft. The witches go to Karonga, or elsewhere, and bring the disease back in a goatskin bag. But not unseen: the ever-watchful dreamers see them, and go out to fight them ; but it would seem that there must be occasions when the powers of good are overcome or outwitted by the powers of evil ; for smallpox does get in ; and the question arises, has it been sent by God, or brought in by wicked persons ? The question is soon answered, for plagues brought in by Divine agency never show a long death-roll: God does not do such things. It is the work of the witches, and the test is administered, and the evil-doers punished. It need hardly be added that the poison test is prohibited, and also the ear test, by European government, and that if it is resorted to at all, it is done in secret. But other methods are in use that are not so easy to detect. A suspected person is mercilessly beaten, and there are many who have, under stress of such thrashings, confessed their guilt, lest the thrashing end in death. In the good old days, before the Europeans began to interfere, guilty persons might be burned to death with all their family. To-day, if the chief is afraid to take more drastic steps, the suspected person is warned to depart. Coming out in the morning he finds at his door a banana stem, with leaves tied to the top ; and if he refuses the hint, he may be mobbed the same day. Native law gives him the privilege of challenging the poison test, and the unhappy chief in that case must either agree and risk being denounced to the magistrate, or refuse to apply the test and withdraw the charge. The lot of the chief who has to steer his way between native and British law is not always a happy one. In the case I am supposing, if he agrees to the poison test in the hope of escaping the attentions of the police, he may find himself with two deaths on his hands, for both accuser and accused must take the test, and although the poison is usually administered in a weak decoction, still accidents have been known to happen.

A plague of mice is also brought on by witchcraft. At Karonga, a man called Ndambasya, still living at Mfuru, on the Rukuru River, possesses this gift. His grandfather was put to death for the offence, but Ndambasya pursues his nefarious practices under the ægis of the British Government, which is far too

R

intelligent to believe such nonsense. The method is
to take a male and a female mouse, cover them up in
a pot with medicines, and when they have bred they
are sent out into the gardens, where they multiply
exceedingly. The British method of dealing with
this plague is to pay so much for every dead mouse
brought in; the Konde believe in getting at the
sources of things, and as the source in this case is
Ndambasya, he, if left to the tender mercies of his
fellows, would die. There was a recrudescence of the
plague in the year 1924, and I suspect Ndambasya
did not feel too comfortable, for the patience of the
people has a habit of coming to a sudden end at times.

The methods by which witches and warlocks work
their evil will are many. By the power of the evil eye
they stop the milk of cattle, bring illness on children,
and cause various kinds of misfortunes to come upon
their enemies. One may kill a man by making a
wax effigy, and letting it slowly melt before the fire.
He will die when the whole has been melted. Pneumonia is brought on by making a small circlet of the
leaves or roots from which various kinds of medicines
are made, and sticking a wooden pin through it. A
banana leaf pinned in four places will lead to the
death of the victim, and the *post mortem* will reveal
four internal wounds. Certain medicines put into a
hole in the ground will turn a blood-red colour.
Cover the hole carefully from sight, and in due time
your man will cease to trouble you. A sure specific
for causing the death of an enemy is made from hair
clippings, nail parings, the spittle, earth gathered from

the footprints of the victim, and the banana or other leaf on which he sat, mixed with medicines of various kinds. The mixture is not administered to the victim. It is enough that it has been compounded.

One more method of operating will be sufficient, though there are many others. The witch or wizard, stark-naked, goes, at night, after all are in bed, to the house of the person he wishes to injure, and there dances the dance called *kuyinga*, and then goes silently away. In the morning a child becomes sick, and shortly dies. Or, if it is not desired to be so unforgiving, the harvest of the victim will be blighted. The wise householder, however, is not without defence. He secures himself and his family, and his gardens, from this kind of thing by placing medicine in the roof of his house, which roots to the spot the dancing wizard, who is found there in the morning, and dealt with.

There is a very complete system of protection, which has been developed during the ages, guarding the person and the community against all kinds of evil, forming, as one writer has remarked, an insurance against accidents and evil powers. The protection against witchcraft is especially complete.

First, there is the risk of discovery by revelation, as in the dreams already referred to ; or by experiment, as when the doctors apply their tests. But although the dreamer sometimes makes his discovery before any evil has been done, he perhaps as frequently fails ; and the doctor is never called in until the evil demands drastic treatment.

Therefore it must be anticipated by the use of powerful medicines, which would probably be called charms in Europe ; but as the Konde call them medicines, I prefer to use that term. There is communal protection, and individual. For the former certain herbs are taken, burned into an ash, and mixed with oil. The mixture is put into two horns, one of which is placed in the rafters inside the chief's house, and the other under the eaves outside, and behind. No one may approach the chief's house from behind, for the medicines would destroy him. But, wheels within wheels, another drug is known which can destroy the efficacy of the drugs in the horn, and therefore anyone seen approaching the house from behind would be suspected of trying to nullify the measures taken to ensure public safety. To make this nullifying drug, the leaves of *malimbalimba* and *undurusya* are taken, and their extract added to what is in the horn, which thereupon loses its virtue, and the public are exposed to danger.

To protect individual houses, the leaves of certain trees are taken, and laid on the fire, so that the smoke, spreading through the house, may ensure the safety of the inmates. Then the same leaves, pounded and mixed with water, are sprinkled on the floor ; and finally the root of another herb is buried under the doorstep, and will effectually prevent the entrance of witch or warlock. When a new house is being built, this same root is placed in various positions in the foundation, and the house is now protected from turret to foundation-stone, and the inmates dwell in security. As already said, no heathen house is without this protection. Gardens and cattle kraals are protected in similar ways.

But witchcraft spreads its nets far and wide, and it is not enough to protect the house, for a man may be attacked outside. To meet this menace, other measures must be taken. Each person drinks a decoction, and swallows a tiny white stone, found only in the Malila district. The effect of this is to enable him to see in dreams any dangers which threaten him personally from witchcraft; and to make assurance doubly sure, some persons wear charms on neck or wrist or ankle.

No one knows when danger will come upon him. One who looks you steadily in the face is probably a wizard; why else should he look at you so? One who does not return your salutation, or returns it half-heartedly; one who denies the reality of witchcraft; one who is a notorious invader of the rights of husbands; all such men (or women) are to be avoided, for they are all probably dangerous.

And the reproach of witchcraft follows one after death. If the *post mortem* shows marks on the internal organs, the person has died of witchcraft; but if the bowels are swollen or blackened, either to the right or to the left, the dead man was beyond doubt himself a wizard; the swollen condition indicates clearly the presence of the two serpents which were the source of his secret powers. Any suspicion that was formerly entertained against him is now confirmed, and his heirs may find themselves involved in demands for reparation.

In 1922 a sorcerer got into the house of the chief Kaloso, near Mwaya. The medicine which is always there brought him to a halt, and when Kaloso rose in the morning, he found him there in the form of an owl! Kaloso is one of the most intelligent chiefs I know; but he sent out word, and his people came in great numbers to see with their own eyes the owl which was a sorcerer caught in the act. The owl was not killed, for who knew what evil might be brought on the district if that were done? I suggested that it was an ordinary owl, which somehow had got into the house the previous evening. But ordinary owls, I was told, do not go into houses, while every one knows that wizards can be changed into owls by the medicine in the chief's house.

Sorcerers have naturally means of self-defence not available for common men. One wounded in a fight licks the wound and recovers; or if the wound is inaccessible to his lips, he takes the blood with his hand and swallows it, with the same result. One who has fallen sick of smallpox licks the pustules and recovers.

CHAPTER XXI

The Powers of Evil: II. Destructive Agencies

THE attack upon Society, if one may so describe it, is not confined to the kind of witchcraft dealt with in the preceding chapter. More terrifying perhaps, and certainly more dramatic, is the power which enables certain persons, also called *Abalosi* (witches, wizards), to call up lions, crocodiles, and other agencies of death, and to direct their operations. When a crocodile secures a human victim, it leaves a part for its " father," the witch or wizard. A person killed by a crocodile, but rescued when too late, is not at once buried ; the body is watched to see if any token of attack by witchcraft can be detected.

More important, however, is the *umperangalamu*, the lion-maker. Let it be again noted that, as in the cases of smallpox, a long death-roll of people killed by a lion is not the act of God ; God does not do such things. It is the work of an evil agent, operating for hire, or to serve his own purposes.

Sir Harry Johnston in his " British Central Africa," tells that when an attack was planned by the British forces upon a certain slave-raiding chief, a friend of the latter, unable to send help in men, sent his son to raise all the lions and leopards in the country against the invaders. So confident were the people of the power of this man, that they did not even go out to fight until the British force was upon them; and even then they made but a faint resistance, believing that the lions and leopards would ultimately come to their aid.

At least three men who claim, or are believed to possess, this power, are alive to-day in or near the Konde country. At Deep Bay, Kayiparule is popularly supposed to have it, and at Fulirwa, not far off, Nkurunganga; both of whom now disclaim knowledge of the secret, though they boast that their fathers knew it.

Kabeta of Musomba village, in the Isoko district, is perhaps the most famous of these men. In 1920 he was hired by a man called Mwamswero to kill men, women, and children in the Nyondo district in Nyasaland. The chief Nyondo was believed to have killed the brother of Mwamswero, and had paid only three cows instead of five to the family of the murdered man. The injured family, having no remedy against the chief, determined to call in other resources, and hence the employment of Kabeta. In the year indicated, a lion killed several people in seven different villages, all belonging to the chief Nyondo, and Kabeta demanded payment. Mwamswero offered him four cows, but the lion-maker demanded five, otherwise Mwamswero himself would be the next victim. In a public inquiry, Kabeta acknowledged

having received the cattle, but admitted that he was
deceiving the people.

There is a medicine which protects those who have
it against these lions. Kabeta himself, on the occasion referred to, gave medicine to the people of
Chinunka, and to the son of Nyondo. To Mwakapalira of Chinunka he gave charms to put on his
neck, and a rod to carry in his hand, with the assurance
that these gave perfect protection to whoever carried
them. One Sunday, Mwakapalira sent his two wives
to the garden to get *malesi* to make beer ; on the way
they met some Christians, who told them that it was
Sunday, and they should not do such work ; but the
women replied that God did not stop working on
Sunday, and in any case they were adequately protected. One of the women was killed within an hour
by a lion, and belief in Kabeta's charms against his
own lions fell to zero.

Individual protection, however, is not enough, and
when such visitations threaten, the chief usually
takes measures for the public safety. The following
is the method practised by the chief Mwenemusuku :
his doctor takes the heart and claws of a lion, which
he boils together with the flesh of the dread flying-
serpent *inyifiwira ;* the chief eats the heart of the
lion, and is assured by the doctor that he is now
himself a lion. The rest of the medicine is powdered
and sent to all the headmen. These send out men to
" walk the marches," bearing some of the medicine,
and praying as they go :

"Ye spirits, be gracious to us. This evil that is
coming upon us, we know not whence it is. If it

is the act of God, let it work, His house is great. But if it is the act of men, let it go where the sin is. I and mine have done nothing amiss."

As they go, they chew, for their own protection, the leaves of a shrub called *munyekomaso*, putting the chewed leaves into a small sack at the side. The common people are warned to go in certain directions only for wood and water as long as the lion is known to be about. When it approaches a village, the local headman speaks :

"You lion, if you have been sent out by men, follow where your prey leads you ; if you are from God, His house is great, go where you will."

Just how much effect this has on the lion, need not, perhaps, be too closely investigated.

There are numerous stories, which, if they do nothing else, illustrate the naïve faith of native Christians in the protecting care of God. A school inspector, going his rounds in 1920, when Kabeta's lion was about, was offered the use of the protecting drugs, but refused. "God Himself," he said, "is my protector." In 1913 an evangelist was followed for some distance by a lion, and at last turned on the brute :

"You lion," he said, "you have no master. I have a Master, Jesus Christ. I do not fear you. Do not follow me ; get off in another direction " ;

which the lion, after roaring angrily, did ! In the same year a lion was moving about on the lake shore, but the Christians, secure in their faith, refused to be kept from their gardens. No one, so far as I heard, either Christian or heathen, was killed at that time. A Christian man, walking alone through the bush, was chased by an elephant. " And God said, ' Look,' and I looked, and behold a pit ; and I went down into it, and the elephant passed me by ; and again God said ' Look,' and I looked, and behold in the pit a very evil snake." There the written report ends ; but as I had myself seen this man holding " a very evil snake " alive in his hand, I have no reason to doubt that he acted with promptitude in the pit.

The *inguluka* is a whitish snake, about four feet long, with a deadly bite. That it should exist at all is bad enough ; but there are sorcerers who create it for their own purposes. Mwankosore, who lives about two miles from me, is believed to possess this power. He takes the roots of the *pusi* tree, which he puts into a pot along with a powerful medicine, and in a little time a snake emerges. The secret of this medicine is known to a very few, and is guarded by word and by spell. The intending purchaser must face a guard of other snakes sent out to kill him by the makers of the drug ; should he, however, kill the snakes, he is acknowledged to be a great doctor, and a supply of the medicine is given to him, for which he pays a cow.

When a sorcerer wishes to kill an enemy, he takes in his hand the snake he has created, and drops it at the house of his intended victim. It immediately makes for the doomed man, strikes, and returns with all speed to its " father." Should the victim have the good fortune to kill it, it will return to its original elements, and appear before him as a mere root of a tree.

The next class of people who possess destructive powers are the poisoners. Direct evidence is naturally hard to get, for the poisoner must act in secret. The poison need not be administered directly, though that is often done ; if placed where the victim will touch it, it is enough ; over the door, where it will drip on his head, or on the threshold, where he will touch it with his foot. Death will follow. In 1905 a man called Ulukamba had a quarrel with a neighbour, and sent his son to place medicine in the doorway of his enemy. Two days later a son of the latter died suddenly. The boy who placed the medicine gave away the secret, by telling some one, and Ulukamba was put to the poison test, which condemned him, and he was ordered to pay over two cows. He refused, threatened to inform the magistrate that the chief had consented to the poison ordeal, and the case had to be dropped. But the belief that he killed the boy is still firmly held by all the people of his village. There was no case against the boy who placed the medicine, as he was obeying orders issued by his father.

The destructive power of anger is firmly believed in by the Konde. To speak the name of a brother in anger, is strictly forbidden, for it may lead to his death. The process is rationalized thus : the spirits hear the words of anger, and, assuming that there is good reason for it, send a disease, or engineer an accident, which kills the person named. A well-known doctor, named Mwenekasangamara, now dead, was credited with wider powers. If he spoke in anger the name of any person within his family, and that was a very wide circle, that person would die. But he had the privilege of withdrawing, and so neutralizing the effect of his anger. The underlying idea is that it is contrary to God's law to speak evil of dignities; if the person spoken against, like Mwene-kasangamara, heard of it, his anger would be aroused, and the spirits would come to his support.

A daughter who despised her father, might be punished with barrenness if her father so desired. Mwenekasangamara imposed this punishment on a married daughter, and the curse was not removed until she had made proper atonement, and soon afterwards her infirmity was corrected. Another well-known case is that of a man called Songwe, living at Lupembe, whose daughter aroused his wrath to such a degree that he called upon his ancestors to destroy her. She became ill the same day, and died the next. This was in December, 1912. In the light of modern psychological beliefs, there is nothing impossible in the story.

CHAPTER XXII

Sickness & Medicine

THE Konde possess a surprisingly wide knowledge of the uses of herbs. I have in my possession a collection of over a hundred specimens of leaves and roots, brought to me by the doctors who used them, and who described to me the disease for which each was a cure, and the manner of applying the drug. Knowledge of these plants is handed down from generation to generation. In a prayer to be given presently, the doctor pleads that he has not departed from the knowledge of his ancestors, as a reason why he should be assisted now ; an attitude which is not, perhaps, a guarantee of progress, but certainly is a guarantee of honesty. The knowledge is quite real so far as it goes. I was myself in 1912 cured instantaneously of a raging toothache by an old native doctor, and two years passed before the trouble returned. The old man boiled in water some rootlets of a tree which grows in the neighbourhood, and the liquid, when cool, was applied to the tooth with a leaf, when the pain vanished as by magic. A few years later another doctor undertook to cure me of a severe attack of neuritis, but I preferred the attentions of a European doctor ; a decision which I have often regretted, not because the European did not cure me, but because I missed an opportunity of testing the native.

A European well known in the country told me recently that in 1901 he was cured of black-water fever by a native doctor on the Zambesi. Water boiled with roasted rice was given him in large quantities, and a small sack, filled with boiled leaves of a tree not known to me, was bound around the abdomen. His recovery was rapid, and he has himself successfully used the same cure in other cases. Another European was cured of persistent dysentery by an old native doctor.

Doubtless there is much pretence ; drugs are administered without real knowledge ; but in the main the doctors are honourable men, fulfilling an important place in the life of the community, relieving much pain, and achieving striking successes, which are too well authenticated to admit of doubt. That in many cases they ruin the patient for life, is unfortunately also only too true. But however that may be, they have not forfeited the confidence of the people. The advent of the scientifically trained European doctor has diminished indeed, but by no means destroyed, the influence of his African confrère in science. Hundreds still consult the native doctor, many in preference to, and not a few after having tried, the white man's medicine. A medical friend of mine tells a good story against himself. He was asked by one of his own employees for the loan of two shillings ; but the applicant was most unwilling to tell what the money was to be used for. It came out, however, that it was to pay a native doctor, to whom he was taking his wife for consultation! The native's fee was two shillings. The fee at the dispensary would not have been one-tenth of that sum, but the patient preferred the high fee and the unqualified adviser. Nor is this surprising, when it is remembered that so much of the troubles which afflict the native, are believed to be due to the interference of spirits, with which the European doctor will have nothing to do ; while the Konde doctor will consult them as part at least, if not the whole, of his diagnosis. Hence the confidence in him. He is in touch with the sources of the trouble.

And this same conviction, that the native doctors are in touch with the sources of the trouble, leads to some of the most foolish beliefs of the common people, and of the most mischievous practices of the doctors. It is the source of the absurd confidence in the power of medicine to turn bullets into water, for example. In 1897 medicine was prepared which would cause the white man, in what was then the Neu Langenburg area, to disappear. It is believed by many natives with whom I have been in touch, that some doctors are seeking for a " formula " to-day, which will succeed where the previous one so obviously failed ; suggestive of a state of mind similar perhaps to that of our own alchemists of centuries ago ; but suggestive also of a desire, at least in some quarters, to see the last of the white man.

Both the gathering of herbs, and the administration

A Prohibitionist.

When food runs low, it is the duty of the chief to prevent undue consumption. The man in the picture has been sent out to prohibit the eating of bananas before a fixed date. He is wearing banana leaves and calabashes. Sometimes he carries a wooden rifle and a bandolier.

of the medicine, is a religious act. Mwenekasanga-mara, the doctor referred to in the previous chapter, used the following prayer, when gathering herbs ; it was given to me by his son, who got it from his father. And Mwenekasangamara claimed that it had descended through many generations in his family.

" Be merciful to me, thou Creator. The medicine which I am seeking is the same that my fathers sought, and it was Thou that didst open their eyes. Show me the roots, and I shall know them. But if my patient is not to recover, hide them from me, and I shall know that it is Thy will."

The following, used when medicine is being administered in a case of ulcer that has resisted treatment, is rather a statement than a prayer :

" If this disease has come from God, medicine will heal it ; for God, who made us, made also the trees, and gave us intelligence to know their properties. But if it has come from men, I cannot heal it."

The last sentence means that witchcraft or the anger of a spirit is at the root of the trouble, and steps must be taken to discover the facts. Then, but only then, the ulcer will yield to treatment.

But behind both the prayer and the medicine, or at any rate in addition to them, there is something else. There are certain medicines which are never administered to patients ; their function is to give power to the doctor himself ; administered to a

s

patient, they would almost certainly kill him, for it is very probable that a patient who believed that he had taken one of these by mistake or otherwise, would die of sheer fright.

The *inyifwira* is a fiery flying-serpent, which lives in pools, and turns the waters red; climbs trees, which thereupon break out into flame, but are not consumed; chases its prey for five miles, and lucky is he whose heels are light enough to escape; and finally, when dead, its body is made into the most powerful drug in the Konde Pharmacopœia. It gives authority to chiefs, and skill to doctors and diviners, and the common man who obtains possession of a tiny quantity is assured of success and riches. To tell the ordinary heathen Konde that all this is fable, is like telling very good and not necessarily unintelligent persons of a few generations ago, that there was no devil, with horns and hoofs and a tail!

Only the biggest doctors undertake to kill this monster when a fresh supply is called for. And even they, before beginning, protect themselves and their assistants with a great variety of other drugs, not so dangerous to obtain. The creature having been located in some pool or other, a small hut is built at a great distance, into which in the past a slave was put, to-day a sheep or a goat. The hut is now clayed over, and closed on all sides, the clay being thickly planted with sharp knives, and the whole sprinkled plentifully with a powdered food, of which the snake is very fond. All being ready, a swift runner is sent to the pool, a bell in his hand, the ringing of which attracts the snake. It emerges from the pool, with a *hu hu* sound, and the runner flies for his life towards the hut, pursued by the snake. Attracted by the sprinkled food, it climbs all over the hut, and is cut to pieces on the knives. After a little, and usually at night, the doctor in charge goes out to reconnoitre, and, finding the dead body, sends to tell all the surrounding chiefs and big doctors ; who come, protected by a powerful prophylactic, for even the dead *inyifwira* can kill the unprotected. Each chief gets a portion of the flesh, a large share going to Chungu, who in turn distributes it to his leading subordinates and doctors. The blood is collected and sold, a small portion for a cow, to smaller men, who have no natural right to it.

The dread in which this medicine (*ifingira* it is now called) is held by the common people, is extraordinary. At Karonga in 1923 a man was accused of attempting to poison another. On his person was found a small packet done up in bark-cloth, which no native in the court would touch ; and when the magistrate took it into his hands and proceeded to open it, the court was cleared in an instant. Whether it was the medicine made from the *inyifwira* snake, I do not know ; but it undoubtedly belonged to that class of medicines.

Illnesses may be due to natural causes, which the native calls God. They yield to treatment without any ceremony. The prayer already quoted indicates the Konde attitude to such diseases. Secondly, illness may be due to witchcraft, and then there is no hope of cure until the sorcerer has been outwitted by the use of both drugs and ceremonies. Next, the action of the spirits brings on diseases, and until the cause of their anger has been dealt with, no doctor will undertake to cure the patient. Wounds or injuries in battle, by falling trees, by attack of animals, or by any other means, may be due to any of the above causes.

The doctor may be a man or a woman. The fee varies from about a farthing to a sixty shilling cow, and the manner of payment varies also. In some cases payment precedes treatment ; in others, it follows ; and in still others the degree of cure effected decides the amount to be paid.

In what follows, no attempt is made at scientific classification ; rather a rough grouping of symptoms guides the sequence of items. Medicines are usually administered in beer or in milk, hot or cold, according to the disease which is being treated. And the place where the decoction is drunk is very important ; in snake bite, for instance, it is fatal for the patient to go inside the house before the medicine has been taken which it is hoped will save his life. A native Christian was, in 1913, suspended from ordinances for drinking medicine while seated on a banana stem at a place where two paths met.

Mental troubles of various kinds are treated, and not, I am assured, without success in some cases. *Maya* is grief, due to any cause. It is treated by giving an infusion of a plant called *nsabe*, not unlike parsley in appearance. The result is great cheerfulness in the patient, due, no doubt, to exhilarating qualities in

the plant. *Ipingu* is sadness, or anger. The parents
or relatives of an absent friend, having no news of him
for some time, give way to grief or anger, and the
emotion causes illness in the absent one. The latter
goes to the diviner to learn why he is ill, and is told.
The leaves of a plant called *inyekenyeke* are pounded
and boiled in water, and the infusion drunk, the
patient saying in the presence of the doctor :

> " Let the words of those people fall back upon
> them. I have spoken no evil ; I am not a hard
> man. God and the spirits behold me. May I get
> sleep."

Minyenya is nightmare. The actual meaning of
the word is *ancestors*, and the bad dreams are due to
their action. It is cured by an infusion of the plant
kateteya, taken while repeating the incantation : " We
drive you away, you who trouble us. Leave our friend
that he may sleep." *Amahelu* is disobedience to
parents or relatives. Take the fruit of *imbangala* and
munyu, and add the flesh of the fish *ingumba ;* reduce
to a powder, and mix with beer in a small calabash.
This the disobedient one is forced to drink three or
four times, nothing being left in the calabash. I have
no doubt at all that most children find obedience less
obnoxious than the mixture. Similar success attends
the use of a drug made from the *mulombwa* tree. The
kasoka is a tiny creature which covers itself with
scraps of grass, and moves by using its head as a lever.
It is a sovereign remedy, when mixed with other drugs,
for madness, as well as for that form of madness which

makes a woman unfaithful to her husband. For *impulamutu*, a brain trouble which makes the sufferer strike his head against trees or other hard objects, there is a cure, but I have not discovered what it is. For dizziness, an infusion is made from the roots of the *kalemerera* plant, and the patient first drinks, then washes his face with, the infusion. Epilepsy is treated with a mixture made from the roots and leaves of many plants. The mouth is forced open if necessary when the drink is being administered. Natives assert that cures are effected, but I know of no cases that have been cured.

There is no disease more common among the Bantu peoples than ulcers, sores, abscesses. The common *kironda* is treated with a wash made from the infusion of pounded *burungo* leaves. If it does not yield to treatment, it is due to witchcraft or spirits, and in either case the necessary preliminaries must be gone through. A special form of this disease is found when the ulcers break out on the breast or in the mouth. The diseased part is washed with an infusion of *indobo* bark, and another infusion is taken internally twice a day for a few days. A more malignant form is called *ndoroka*, for which the leaves of the plant *kanga* are infused, and applied as for *kironda*, with the same ceremonies, if a cure is not effected within a reasonable time. *Mpenga* is a slightly different form of *ndoroka*. *Kabimba* is something of the nature of an inside tumour which must be let out. Roots of the *tubimba* shrub are reduced to a dry powder, spread on the leaf of the *untugutu* tree, and bound to

the place with a cord made from fibre of *kabumbu*;
in about ten minutes the swelling will burst and the
matter escape. The same results follow from binding
the place with cord made from *unguluka* shrub.
Gourds are often used instead of leaves, and are tied
on with cords passing through holes bored in the
sides of the gourd. For syphilis (*kaswendi*) the roots
of the *indabi* shrub are infused and drunk, and a
powder made from *indobo* shrub is rubbed into the
wounds or sores.

Kitasya is intussusception of the bowels, found
mostly in children, and usually fatal. When one child
after another in a family dies, an examination is made
of the bowels, bamboo knives being used for the
operation. If *kitasya* is indicated, the parents drink
an infusion made from the leaves of a creeper called
inguluka, which is taken with beer. Then the bed is
turned so that the head is where the feet were. The
woman wears on her neck, tied up in a piece of bark,
a section of the plant from which the infusion is made.
But in giving this medicine, as in many others, the
doctor will say, " This medicine is not mine ; it is
God's ; He must work in you." When another child
is born, the doctor is called to give it medicine, and
to shave its head. The fee is a cow ; and a hoe is paid
when the child reaches the age of three.

For other internal conditions, a mere enumeration
must suffice. Internal pains, dysentery, diarrhœa,
constipation, worms, vomiting, indigestion, and was-
ting diseases are all treated in similar fashion, each
having its own specific drug or mixture of drugs.

Fever, if due to natural causes, is treated with the infusion of the leaves of *amafumbo* ; if due to the action of the spirits, a prayer for mercy is added. *Sekema* is malaria with headache. The patient must sit in the open, where he can see the sun, and drink from a closely woven basket an infusion of *lusisigembe* ; and in some cases the extracted juice of *moromoro* is put into one ear. There is a " general sickness " called *bukanye*, due to witchcraft. To neutralize the witch-craft, the whole body is washed with an infusion of *ulukanganunya*, and a drink is given made from the leaves of the *mungwina* tree. Severe burning is gener-ally believed to be the work of the spirits if it occurs at night, and it is at night that most burns occur. The native is a heavy sleeper, and he lies with his feet stretched out towards the fire. A brand falls upon a foot, and he is burned before he has properly awakened ; but it was the work of the spirits, who have now to be placated with cloth, or a goat, or a fowl. Then the burned parts are smeared with the honey of a small insect called *umunya*, and washed with the infusion of the leaves of the *kasambanya* shrub. Scalding is treated with castor oil.

Muscular pains like *ikiraso* and *ilyuru*, which are probably pneumonia and rheumatism, are treated first as due to natural causes, and if this fails, witch-craft is assumed to be the cause, and steps taken accordingly. Prayer is offered, if the following can be called prayer :

" You *kiraso*, if you have come from God, the medicine will cure you. If you have been sent by men, are not they also flesh? They fail, they die; but first they kill us. Let this disease fly away from me."

An infusion of the roots of *indobo* tree already mentioned, is now given to the patient.

Diseases of the eyes, ears, teeth, gums are also treated. A list would be tedious, and a detailed statement there is no space for. Enough to say that a person qualified for the task could write a good-sized book on the subject of native medicine. There are, however, still some diseases and practices of which some brief account must be given.

Snake bite. Naturally in a land where snakes are numerous, antidotes are in use, and are claimed to be successful. The roots of *kisongora* infused and drunk, are said to be a sure remedy, if taken in time. A rich man, however, would not be advised to take this alone, for his riches bring him under suspicion of being a sorcerer, and the snake may have bitten him by command of his jealous fellow-sorcerers. To overcome this an incantation must be used.

"May you be defeated! The goods I have, I stole from no man. They are my own. This is true, as God sees me."

Another remedy is the root of *kitumbo*, the infusion mixed with soot from the inside of the house. The mixture must be drunk outside, for if the patient goes in he will die. A method favoured by other doctors is to hold the part bitten over a fire to which has been added the leaves of the *unkwesi*, a large tree. Presently the fang will drop out, and the man will be saved! There are men living near me who claim to have seen this being done.

The birth of children is accompanied by loving care, gross superstition, and much medical treatment, useful or otherwise. All women at that time are given a drink of *indobo* leaves, pounded and mixed with water. If the placenta has not come away satisfactorily, castor oil is given. And if pain supervenes, the bark of *indobo* is again given, pounded and mixed with water. For a child weak at birth, roots of *unsuba* and *mungwina* are taken, pounded, mixed with water, and the child is washed in the mixture. Sterility in man or woman can be removed by the right drugs; and when a woman is getting on in years and wishes no more children, a mixture is in use which will have the desired effect. Medicines for producing abortion are widely known, and frequently used, as also are love potions.

Steaming is resorted to in cases of great pain or weakness. Water is cooked in a large pot, with the bark of *mparampara* added. When the pot has boiled, it is taken off the fire, and the patient, covered with a mat, kneels over it, supported if very weak, for about ten minutes. Massaging also is employed when one is very tired, the leaves of *muyoka* being pounded to give a juice for lubrication, or, as the people themselves say, to get into the body through the pores. Cupping is employed for headache and rheumatic pains. Eight cuts are made in two lines, on each side of the head; a small horn is put over the cuts; a vacuum is created by suction, and the hole in the horn closed with beeswax. In about a quarter of an hour the cup is removed. Pain in the eyes, legs, back, is so treated.

Smallpox, the most dreaded of all scourges, has already been dealt with under "Worship" and "Witchcraft," and all that is here necessary is to indicate what is done for the cure of patients. An infusion made from the roots of *ikanganunya* and *sambwe* is given to drink, and the body is washed with the same mixture. The pustules are opened with the thorns of *unsuba*. But more important than the medicine is a clear conscience in the patient; and prayer to the spirits and confession of sins must be made before the medicine is administered. The father, in the presence of all the family, says : " My son has small-pox ; let us be at peace ; whoever has anything against him, let him declare it." Any matters against the sick man are now inquired into. It may be a debt, or a quarrel, or a charge of impudence in the case of a boy. The sick man is also questioned, and makes his confession, usually of misconduct with girls, who are forbidden to approach the house. If married women are involved, neither they nor their husbands may come near. A prayer for the removal of the disease is now offered by the family representative, at the door of the house in which the patient lies, and the prayer is accompanied by the usual squirting of water from the mouth, which is never omitted. The medi-cine may now be administered to the sick man. A prophylactic is used by all the other members of the family who have not had smallpox, but it is evidently not greatly trusted, for it is used with the formula, " Protection against smallpox is unknown, but let us try. If God and the spirits agree we shall be safe." After this ceremony there must be no quarrelling. Peace in the village is a condition of immunity from the disease.

In a considerable number of cases incisions are made in the skin, and powdered medicine rubbed in. This is done for general pains, rheumatism, backache, elephantiasis, toothache, spleen. For toothache, if the pain is in the right side of the face, incisions are made between the great and second toes of the left foot, and the powder rubbed in ; if the pain is in the left, the powder goes in the same way into the right foot.

Post mortems are still conducted in all cases where there is any doubt as to the cause of death. Until quite recently no one was buried without examination, and in some districts that is still the case. The operation is performed at the graveside by the friends of the dead man, the actual operator being as a rule a near relative. If a black substance is found in the gall-bladder, a diviner is consulted, to find out who brought on the disease. If the examination of the gall-bladder yields no result, the heart is examined. Ulcers on that organ indicate witchcraft as the cause of death ; fat indicates leprosy. Next, the intestines are examined ; if *mafira* (pus) is found there it indicates a kind of rheumatism accompanied with boils. The examination being over, the parts removed are restored to their places, and the body is buried ; and all who had any part in the operation drink medicine to protect them from the disease from which the man died.

For wounds in battle an infusion of the roots of *kamemena* is given to cause vomiting, in case there is blood in the stomach. The wounds are washed with an infusion of *impigi* roots, and bound with leaves of *untugutu*, fresh dressings being applied every day until the wounds are healed.

CHAPTER XXIII

Wonder Medicine

NOT that the Konde wonders; he wonders at the achievements of the European; but his own far greater marvels do not rouse his curiosity. They are part of the order of Nature, and no more matter for surprise than the effects of medicine administered directly to a patient. Through long generations they have known men who had power to stop the rain, or to cause the wind to blow, or to do other things which common men cannot do. Where is the difficulty in believing these things? Is it true that the white man does not even believe what he sees taking place before his eyes? " *Imbulukutu yo syola*," the ear is a deceiver, indeed, but you must either believe what you see before you, or give up all pretence of sanity. Coincidence? It is just as easy to say God, and a great deal more sensible; for it is God who gives to each man his powers; to one, power to cause the wind to blow; to another, power to bring lions and leopards; to another, power of witchcraft, and so on. In every case medicine is used, but, to repeat what was said in the preceding chapter, "God, who made man, made also the trees, and gave us intelligence to know their properties."

One of my native friends, when on a journey,

chews, as he goes, a certain root; and he fears no
wild animal, for none will come near him. The secret
has been in his father's family for generations, and
not one of them was ever killed by a wild animal.
Another incises powdered medicine into his wrists
and ankles, and he is absolutely free from danger of
snakes. Nor has it ever been heard of that a man
wearing certain charms on his ankles while crossing
a river, has been taken by a crocodile. Men have been
taken by crocodiles from time to time, but they were
either too poor to buy this charm, or too foolish to
wear it. It is all law, though the Konde knows nothing
about what we call law. Get the right medicine, and
the desired result is sure: that is law. Perform the
correct ceremonies, and what you ask for will come,
as sure as water will come through an open pipe:
that also is law. But it does not follow that the
native will accept anything that is offered him as a
charm. He must know who made it, where the maker
got his knowledge, what is his ancestry. Any proof
will not do. It must be proof that will satisfy the
Konde; and that is by no means what would satisfy
a white man. But the obstinacy with which the white
man refuses to believe in things that to the African
are so obvious as hardly to call for explanation, is
part of the reason why still the latter has doubts as
to the perfect sanity of the European. One who does
not comprehend the obvious is mentally below par.

In preceding chapters native beliefs and practices
in regard to various illnesses, agriculture, war, lions,
hunting and fishing, have been indicated.

One of the commonest charms is called *isigita*, and is worn on neck, wrist, or ankle, as a protection against snakes, crocodiles, lions, or leopards. It guards also against sore eyes, ulcers, evil spirits. This powerful charm, the description of which reads like a patent medicine advertisement, is made as follows : take dry *pupwe* or *mphiyi* roots, reduce to powder, add powdered head of *kitumbi* snake, and a piece of *mphiyi* root ; set the whole to boil on the fire in a broken pot. Then cut the roots into four pieces, string them on cords, leave two such cords in the house, and carry another wherever you go. If bitten by a snake, chew quickly at the charm, and then bind it on the wound.

When crossing a river, this charm, strung as before, is tied to the legs, the four pieces in this case hanging at about three inches from each other. Numerous other charms are used for the same purpose, but the one I have described is the favourite.

Children suffering from mumps take small bundles of firewood, and lay them at the cross-roads, where the first passer-by will pick up the disease, and the children will immediately recover.

A youth who finds himself unpopular with maidens, goes to the doctor, who incises a powder between the eyes in the forehead. His unpopularity will assuredly pass away, as will that of a girl similarly treated. An older man who is disliked or distrusted by his fellows, has a different medicine incised into the same place, and with equal success. But, more valuable still, a man who is involved in a lawsuit, before either the magistrate or the local chief, or who wishes to gain

A DEATH DANCE.

The dance is in honour of the dead person, and is not seldom an unrestrained orgy of emotion let loose. If spear and shield are carried, fighting may take place, ending in wounds and death, especially at the burial of a chief, who should not go to his ancestors unattended.

the favour of the white man for any reason, can be supplied with a charm which will secure the end he has in view. For a few moments after the interview begins, he chews at the charm, then removes it from his mouth, trusting for the rest to what has been incised in his forehead. A favourable result may be confidently expected.

Thieving charms are also in use, and men who operate under such protection are called *balebi*. A drug unknown to me is tied up in a leaf, and thrown on to the roof of the house to be robbed, and also at the door, to make the inmates sleep. The thieves enter, either by opening the now facile door, or by digging ; and immediately place another drug under the heads of the sleeping owners of the house. " May they sleep heavily ; may they dream dreams," is their incantation. Another medicine is worn on the wrists. So bold are the robbers thus protected that, when they have removed everything they wish, they awaken the sleepers, and demand food (which is given to them), without fear of being recognized ; but it is not per-haps surprising, considering the fear in which these criminals are held, that the victims never admit that they recognize the thieves.

The house, however, may be protected. Powdered root of *ikitebo* is spread all over the house, and any thief who enters will have sores breaking out on his lips, a thing which happens only to thieves who have ignored this charm.

Kondeland should be a paradise for debtors, for the man who knows the ropes can arrange to put off pay-

T

ment so often that finally it is either not paid at all,
or paid when it is quite convenient for the debtor to
do so. To secure this desirable result the debtor,
when he learns that his creditor is coming to demand
payment, slips out into the bush, where he gets the
roots of a plant called *butisi*, which he chews as the
creditor approaches. A most amiable conversation
ensues, at the end of which the creditor begs his
friend on no account to disturb himself about the
small matter that lies between them : any other time
will do just as well, and he will be delighted to call
again in a couple of months or so. The same end is
attained by incising a powder into the forehead
between the eyes.

Hunting medicines have already been referred to.
One is incised along the bone from the thumb to the
elbow ; another is taken internally, but this latter is
dangerous, because it leads to a lingering death. When
death draws on, instead of dying as common men do,
the whole body of the hunter who drinks this medicine
becomes helpless ; the heart keeps going, the lips move
and talk ; death does not come. Then his friends
come and sing to him : " *Ndembo syaya mmiyombo*,"
the elephants are among the trees. The sick man,
puffing out his cheeks, emits breath with a whirring
sound, which is supposed to resemble a sound made
by elephants, and presently he breathes his last.

But there are few ills, imaginary or otherwise, for
which there are no cures, imaginary or otherwise :
and the cautious hunter, finding old age creeping on
him, and his hunting days becoming a thing of

memories and yarns, eats food made from the flour of a pumpkin, which destroys the virtues of his hunting medicines, and at the same time takes away all probability of his death being the prolonged weariness it would otherwise be.

Fishing nets are drugged to ensure a good catch; but here again caution must be exercised, for a very great catch is an omen of a very large family, which is not always an ambition held by the Konde people.

The mother who has just given birth to a child must not cook food, nor may she warm herself at the common fire; a small fire is kindled for her at which she sits by herself; and when the child goes out of the house for the first time a medicine is put into its mouth to guard it against the ills of the world into which it has come.

Christians do none of these things; but Christians are not as other people. They have passed away from the fear of spirits and from the dread of a world in which anything may happen at any moment; and the fact that they escape the consequences of failure to follow custom is having its effect on the common people, many of whom are cautiously experimenting to see whether they too may live a freer and more unshadowed life; but the belief in the protective powers of such things as I have been describing dies hard.

CHAPTER XXIV

Death & Burial

AMONG the Konde, as among other Bantu peoples, no man dies " unwept, unhonoured, or unsung." However contemptible he may have been in life, he has now passed to a sphere in which he is clothed with fresh powers, which, for good or ill, he can direct upon his living descendants, who take care to give no cause of offence. He cannot, however, punish them for any evil they may have done him while alive ; only *post mortem* sins can be visited upon them : neglect of ceremonies, refusal of beer at the funeral, omission of his name when prayer is made, and other tokens of forgetfulness. And the power for harm of each spirit is limited to his own descendants ; but chiefs, naturally, can bring misfortune upon the whole of the community over which they ruled in life.

Immediately a man has died, his eldest child, son or daughter, unless an infant, begins the mourning.

"Alas, my father, I too have met trouble ! " Then the women, "Ah ! trouble comes to you as to others." Next the leader, " My father, my lion, my leopard," naming all the strong and fierce animals to which the dead man is compared ; the women say, " Now indeed you are poor " ; and the boy replies, " Yes, my

292

mothers, my strength is gone, my hope is broken. How poor am I among men!" If he is a boy he is now taken by a kindly relative and put outside, and told not to weep like a woman. During all this time, and perhaps for three days to come, the drum is beating; a slow tum tum at first, but rising later to a more furious noise, which goes on night and day until the mourning is over.

The women now take up the tale, and one goes over all the virtues of the dead, a long wail from the others following upon each statement. Day by day this goes on, as new parties come to the mourning. The women smear their bodies and their faces with clay, and wear bands of banana fibre or of palm leaf on ankles, wrists, and forehead. The men, at the death of an important person, carry spear and shield.

In the meantime some relatives have gone to dig the grave, and others are dressing the dead man for burial. The body is washed, a man's body by men, and woman's by women, and dressed in *manyeta* (body rings), anklets, wristlets, and finally swathed in as much cloth as his relatives can afford to buy, only the eyes being left uncovered. Before the dressing, however, the body is oiled, and if the dead man was a warrior, his *isambanjuni* (feather head-dress) is placed on his head.

The women now take up the body, and carry it through the village, wailing as they go. Having shown the dead man for the last time around the familiar haunts of his life, they lay him down near the grave, where mats are spread to receive him. Now the *post mortem* takes place, though in the neighbourhood of Missions and Magistracies the practice is beginning to die out. Only the operators are present, and when it is over the others approach again. The brothers or near relatives of the dead man go down into the grave and receive the body from other relatives who hand it to them. It is not placed in the bottom of the grave, but in a cavity dug into the side, the entrance to which is closed with a bamboo door, before the soil is filled in. The body faces towards the original home of the dead. If the dead man possessed cattle, a curious ceremony now takes place. A cow is brought, and made to look into the grave where her late owner lies, her head being forcibly bent if necessary. The cow is now the property of the spirits, and must never be given away or sold out of the family. Little children of the dead man are handed across the grave, and older children leap over it, and then pull themselves, in a sitting position, over the soil which is presently to be filled in. If this ceremony is properly performed, the dead parent will not disturb the children by nightmares. Its omission is an insult to the dead ; but the practice is being abandoned by the more progressive sections of the community. It is at this point that the parting address, given in the chapter on " The Spirits," is spoken. When the soil is filled in, a cutting of *indola* tree is placed at head and foot, to mark the grave.

All who took any part in the burying must now wash in running water, which carries off the pollution ; and carries off also the danger of the disease which killed the man passing over to those present at the funeral. Those who performed the *post mortem* take medicine as well. The funeral ox or cow is now killed, and the flesh divided among the various groups. The next stage is to " disinherit " the dead man, to cut him off from all connection with earthly matters. His mats were buried with him ; now his bananas are cut down, his hoes are taken to the grave and the hafts broken, while all baskets and pots are destroyed and left to rot there. His cattle go to his heirs, and his wives build themselves huts in which they live for a year, " covering the footsteps of the dead man " ; after which they also go to the heirs. (Much of this is now falling into disuse, especially around Karonga.) The dead man has been dissociated from the living : the bananas grow again, but they are not his ; his house may be occupied, but he has only the rights of a ghost in it ; and in many places the house is left to decay as soon as the funeral is over, and the wives have built themselves huts not far off. But the belief also prevails, side by side with the desire to cut off the dead man from the living, that by destroying his goods they go with him to the land of spirits.

The Konde have a strange belief, that a dead body casts no shadow ; if it does, it is a sign that the spirit still lingers around, and if he is not driven off, another member of the family will die soon. The most effective way of despatching him to his proper abode is to burn his body. If the diviner finds that a second death in the family is due to the reluctance of the first to go to his fathers, the body is dug up, and medicine placed in the empty grave, which attracts the lizard into which the soul of the dead man has entered. It is thus caught and burned in the grave. The parents or near relatives drink medicine, and the body is carried off by the doctor to be burned in the bush. Among the Bandali, all bodies are dug up after the flesh has rotted away, and the bones are taken into the forest, where they are placed in a sitting position against a tree and left there. A much more gruesome custom, which prevails among the Bandali, is that of keeping the bones on the verandah of the heir's house, done up in banana leaves, which are renewed as required, the bones being occasionally anointed with oil. Here and there throughout Konde-land are places called *Itago*, so named from the verb *kutaga*, to cast away. In the long past, when a man was dying, and all hope of recovery had been abandoned, he was carried to the *Itago*, placed in a sitting position, and left to die. After death the flesh was devoured by birds or beasts. Nowhere, so far as I have discovered, is this repulsive practice now followed.

The death dance begins as soon as the first wailing is over, and continues as long as people continue coming in to mourn. The men carry spears or sticks, if the dead man was of any importance ; the women have leaves or tails. When the dance has fully developed, the men form one line, and the women another, facing them. The two lines approach each other, the men raising their spears and shields, the women waving the leaves or tails ; at about a yard apart they retire again, shouting or singing as the drum

VARIOUS MOVEMENTS IN THE DEATH DANCE.

The performers advance at a run to a fixed line, then retire, waving spears,
or clubs, shouting and singing, while the drums beat out their persistent
tum tum. Individuals rush about alone, brandishing weapons, and other
mourners are keening the death song in or near the house of the deceased.

beats out its monotonous noise. In the meantime there may be uncontrolled persons running about, leaping, waving spears, not seldom casting a taunt, which is quickly taken up, and spears are thrown, and wounds, and even death, may be the result.

Sometimes the wailing takes place in the house, or in the open, just outside. It is interesting to watch men and women approach the place of mourning : they come with all appearance of *sang-froid*, but suddenly emotion grips them, and they take up the wail with streaming tears. It does not occur to anyone that he should restrain himself ; it was not for that that he came. Yet the recovery from this high-pitched emotion is just as rapid. There is a sudden hush, some one addresses to the widow the old, world-old, world-wide comfort, that all must die ; and, amazing to relate, this is often received with laughter, not mocking laughter, but laughter intended to re-lieve the strain which all are feeling. Sometimes too, jesting, and even obscene language, are indulged in, with the same end in view. And as emotion rises again, and this especially among the dancers, free rein is given to looseness of language and gesture, and more definite evil follows in the darkness.

It is affirmed that all this looseness has arisen since the coming of the white man ; but statements of the harm done by the latter are so common among the Konde and other tribes, that one may well be sceptical. The explanation given is that European government will not permit the old death penalty for adultery, and therefore it has become more common ; or that the number of cattle has increased so greatly since European administration commenced, that there are many who can pay the fine imposed ; or again, that since civilized government will not permit the fighting that used to take place, the emotion generated has to find other outlets.

As parties from a distance come to the mourning, they go first to the " owner " of the dead, and offer their sympathies. In return they are given a long account of the progress of the disease, and of the measures that were taken by relatives to prevent death. A man approaching a widow, will sit at a distance of about a yard to offer his condolences, but a woman throws her arms around the neck of the bereaved.

The Konde do not attach the same value to life as we do, and suicide is not uncommon. I have known of suicide due to small money troubles, loss of a law-suit, continued poverty, prolonged illness, leprosy, quarrels at home, and finally to disappointment in love ; this last, I am told, only on the part of the man ; a woman disappointed in love does not commit suicide. For people who die by their own act, there is less mourning than for an ordinary death, and the parting words at the graveside are not the same ; " since it was by your own desire that you went." The spirits require an explanation from every one who comes to them in this way ; but any answer seems to satisfy them. Ordinarily the new-comers are received with the words, "Come and rest." This information comes from persons who " died " and returned, though a more common belief is that the dead do not return.

Lepers are now buried like ordinary persons. But in the not very distant past, they were placed in a sitting position against a tree, and so left to be devoured. No one of those who carried the body looked behind, lest he also should be " caught " by the disease.

About a month after the funeral, the beer feast takes place. A small quantity is taken to the grave, and the dead man is addressed, and bidden again to go to his ancestors. " Take this beer as an offering to them. The ox that we have killed is also for them." The day is given up to eating and drinking, with intervals of wailing, the men in the open, the women in the house of the heir, or near relative of the dead man.

The ceremonies for women and children are similar to those described. A small chief, near Karonga, who was utterly neglectful of his mother during her life, impoverished himself in the splendour of her funeral. The grave was completely lined with expensive cloths, and the body was decked out as it never had been in life. The man's grief was genuine ; or if it was not grief, it was fear of what the old lady, with her renewed powers, might do, if he did not attend to her now that she was dead.

When the mourning is over, all the friends of the dead man shave their heads. Omission of this ceremony involves the careless one in a quarrel with the departed.

Here and there throughout the country ancient customs survive which have been dropped by the majority of the people. In many places the entrance of the heir upon his new position is accompanied by strange ceremonies. He is taken hold of by the men, and the wives of the dead by the women, and put into the house, the women being told that this man is now their husband. Presently they come out again, and the man is garlanded with leaves, and his head covered with ashes. When all have washed in running water or in the lake, another ceremony must be gone through. Bananas and small beans are roasted, and the company, led by the doctor, move out on their hips to the road, where the doctor digs a small hole, into which he inserts a banana, and into the banana a bean. One by one the people come up, and stooping down, eat the banana without touching it with their hands, a fresh banana being placed for each until all have eaten. Next, with a white fowl and a bunch of bananas, all go to the stream or the lake, where the fowl and the bananas are dipped twice, and each goes in on hands and knees, completely submerged, turns right round, and comes out again. The wives now go each to her father, to inform him that they have a new husband, and the latter sends to each of his fathers-in-law a gift of a hoe.

In the family of the Nyangomale, the heir washes all the children of the deceased, big or little, by pouring water upon their outstretched hands, himself keeping as far off as he can, for none of the water must touch him. He and his new wife, or wives, are now bound together by the thumbs with bark-cloth, and go to the stream, where they wash, and throw away the bark-cloth which bound them. A feast follows.

The Bakifuna go to the stream to wash, garlanded with flowers, and carrying a small stone. Flowers and stone are thrown into the stream after the washing, and the company re-enter the house. The doctor takes water and pours it on the roof, upon which all come out one by one, the water dripping on each as he or she passes. Anointed with oil, they all go to the place of burial, where, resting on elbows and knees, they draw themselves along the grave, slightly disturbing the soil as they go. The hair is then cut, and the feast follows.

When a chief is *in articulo mortis*, his headmen and his wives are present, and he is addressed, while still living, as common men are addressed at the graveside. "Go to God and the spirits; go to your fathers (naming them). Rest there, and tell them what is happening here above."

After he is dead, the nails of his fingers and toes are clipped, and his hair cut, and given to the doctor, who will make medicine with them to prevent the disease which killed the chief passing over to others. The dead man is now dressed as common men are dressed for burial, but much more elaborately, and, if he is a relative of Chungu, he is placed in a sitting position in the house, where his wives and headmen embrace him for the last time. If he is a very important chief, like Chungu, his death is not yet announced to the people.

Meantime a cow has been killed at the place where the body is to be buried, and the headmen dig the grave, usually by night, if intimation has not been made that the chief is dead. The body is brought to the grave by the headmen, and the dead cow is lowered in first ; then the chief, in a sitting position, facing the Sango country, if that was his original home. Torches are used if the night is dark. When the grave is filled in, all partake of the medicine made from the dead man's nails and hair. The washing ceremonies are the same as for common men ; but the widows will not go near the men who placed the body in the grave until the latter have given them a gift of some kind, though the exact function of the gift is not clear.

No chief of any importance dies a natural death : that is to say, however and whenever a chief dies, it is assumed that some one was responsible. It is believed that chiefs die more easily than common men, and are more open to evil influences ; but, on the other hand, they have more powerful medicines to protect them. When Kabeta died in 1922, all his sons and his headmen were put to the poison test, and those who did not vomit were compelled to pay a fine in cattle, a token that complete confidence in the belief in evil influences is passing away ; for in earlier times the culprit so discovered would have been attacked as he ran, and would probably have paid the forfeit of his own life. The easier punishment may, however, have been due to fear of the police.

Twins were not exposed ; but if one of them died, the body was cast into the bush, and wailing was not permitted, for it would cause the death of the other. To-day the body of a twin is buried in the ordinary way, but without wailing.

CHAPTER XXV

The Brave Days of Old

LIKE the Romans and Greeks, and like many
peoples at an elementary stage of civilization,
the Konde place their great days in the past.
It is, perhaps, a little strange that this should
be so ; for there can be no doubt that the presence
of the white man has stirred the African everywhere
to the thought of a new day for his race. But they
are at the same time conscious that great things were
done in the past, and among the demands made upon
me by natives whom I have consulted, and who have
helped me with this book, there is none more insistent
than that I should include the portentous happenings
of an older day.

Old and middle-aged men speak gleefully of the
days of their youth ; of the great deeds they did when
they were boys ; how they trapped more skilfully,
caught bigger fish, ran faster, leaped higher than the
young men of to-day. And the deterioration, they
assert very emphatically, is due to the presence of
the white man. Not that the latter discourages
sport ; on the contrary he spurs it on ; but in his
own way, and that is not the Konde way. The white
man's way is to give prizes to the winner ; the Konde

way is to give the lash to the duffers ; and they claim
that theirs is the more effective method of bringing
all up to a high standard.   But thrash the ninny to-day,
and he is off to the Administrative Officer to lodge
his complaint, which the latter must inquire into.
And hence much deterioration.

But these are not the facts of which they wish a
permanent record to be made.   There are other
things ; things which the pagan native profoundly
believes, and which Christians also believe and take
pride in, though they think that the missionary will
object to their holding what he probably calls silly
ideas.   These stories include most of the typical tales
of olden times :   the hero-warrior, the defier of
tyrants, the mighty medicine man, the great prophet,
the man who has obtained lordship over Nature in
some form, and the man who controls the spirits.   All
these, and many more, are included among the Konde
tales, and I do not place them among folk tales, for
the people regard them quite differently.   A folk tale
is to-day, whatever it may have been in the past,
either a mere diversion to pass away an idle moment,
or a moral for children, or a warning for adolescents.
The tales which I am thinking of are, in the native
mind, records of facts, facts which they believe to be
no longer achievable, but indubitably fact in the past ;
and no study of the native mind can be complete
which does not take this into account.

I. The hero-warrior.   Chungu, in his early wan-
derings in search of a home, came near the hil
Mphande, the seat of the Simbove rulers of that day.

Like the English King Alfred, he determined to be his own intelligence department, and, scouting around for the best point of attack, he came upon a woman working alone in the fields, gathering *makuka*, heaps of grass to be burned before the hoeing.

"Who," he asked the woman, "are the dwellers on that hill?"

"Are you a stranger here," she replied, "that you do not know that that is the hill of the Simbove?"

"I am going there now," said Chungu; "if they pursue me I will come to you, and you shall hide me in the grass heap. If they ask for me you shall say that you know nothing, and if they put you to the poison test, you will be acquitted."

Setting out again, Chungu crept up the stronghold of which he was soon to be master; but he was observed, and presently came rushing back to claim the woman's help. Scarce was the grass well over him ere his enemies broke in with threatening spears, demanding the immediate surrender of the spy. The woman boldly kept her secret, and the poison test having acquitted her, the Simbove set fire to the grass heap by which they were standing, and in which Chungu lay concealed, and went on in their pursuit. How Chungu escaped from the fire must be left to conjecture, but one remembers that he was "the man who speaks with God."

He now brought up a herd of elephants, which when the Simbove saw, they crowded out with spears to the kill; and the invading chief drove the elephants far off, so that all the men of warrior age were drawn away

U

from the defence. Next he brought up a flock of guinea-fowl, and all the old and the feeble, and the women and children, went out after them, only to be drawn away as the men were. Chungu now gave the signal to his warriors, who rushed upon the place, seized it without opposition, and beat the great drum to apprise the whole land that a new lord ruled at Mphande.

II. The defier of tyrants. Long ago there was a chief called Mwambagi. When he killed an ox, he called up all his people, bidding them cut up the animal, and cook the feast in great pots. But when all was ready, he ordered them off to their homes, and sat down to devour the food with his favourites, while the hungry people, with the savour of the well-cooked feast in their nostrils, went sadly to their homes. Next day the tyrant went round among his people.

" I hope you enjoyed the feast yesterday," he leered.

" O yes, sir," they answered, " it was very good indeed."

But there was one man, Kasanda by name, who refused to be humbugged any longer; and when one day, after the people had suffered this grievous disappointment, the chief came round to receive their hungry and disgusted plaudits, the trouble began.

" Did you enjoy the feast yesterday," demanded the chief.

" What feast ? " boldly asked Kasanda. " When did you give us a feast ? "

" I feasted you yesterday," said the angry tyrant.

" You may have feasted others," was the reply, " but I came back hungry."

The enraged bully ordered his men to arrest and bind the rebel, and throw him over a precipice called "Ikisyo." But as he was falling over, Kasanda found that the ropes that bound him untied of their own accord ; and as he rolled downwards, the precipice became a gently sloping descent, over which he fell without harm. The chief was amazed.

"How has he escaped?" he anxiously asked his attendants. But they merely shrugged their shoulders.

"Call to him," said the chief, "and tell him that I have erred."

So Kasanda, unharmed by his adventure, walked up the sloping ascent, which had been a precipice, and which became a precipice again as soon as he reached the top, where the chief and his attendants awaited him. To settle the quarrel, the chief gave his daughter to Kasanda, along with four cows, and no more demanded praise for good deeds not done. "And all the people praised Kasanda, saying, 'Thank you.' Such was the cruelty of Mwambagi, and such the courage of Kasanda."

III. The people take a pride in the great doctors of the past ; for it is the doctors, and not the prophets, who are the miracle workers. The Hebrew prophets sometimes appeared to control Nature, but in all cases it was the act of God, who intervened at the prayer of the prophet. In the Konde stories the doctor does not pray for Divine intervention, nor are his acts regarded as anything but the expression of his own powers.

There were two great doctors, Kasekenye and

Gwasa, of equal skill, and deadly rivals in their art. One day at a beer feast, a dispute arose, in the presence of the two, as to which of them was the greater, and a challenge was issued. Gwasa made medicine, and called upon the people to observe the result. Presently the sun began to sink towards the earth, and the people cried out in terror ; but at a sign from Gwasa it retreated again, and resumed its accustomed place in the heavens. It was now Kasekenye's turn. Plucking a shrub from the ground, he revealed to the astonished gaze of the people a beautiful village of the underworld, men going about, or lying in the sun, cattle feeding in the meadows, trees and rivers, hills and valleys, just as the fathers had told them of the life of the underworld. He replaced the shrub, and the vision vanished. And no man could tell which of these two wonders was the greater, that of Gwasa, or that of Kasekenye.

But trouble came upon the community. The cattle became thin, sorcerers abounded, and evil fell upon all the people ; and the chief called upon the two doctors for help. Each sprinkled the ground with his chosen medicine ; but Kasekenye, hoping to steal a march upon his rival, sprinkled another medicine by night. But he was punished. His body broke out into sores, and he was fain to call in his rival to cure him, and the superiority of Gwasa was acknowledged. But one minor chief was not satisfied. He called upon Gwasa to come and cure him of a pretended illness. The angry doctor, immediately perceiving the trap, threw his medicine bag against the wall of his patient's house, where it stuck, and he stalked wrathfully off. The gift of an ox calmed his wounded spirit, and he removed the medicine bag from the wall. "Then did all men know that Gwasa was a great doctor."

IV. Occasionally others besides doctors controlled aspects of Nature. Ntindi was a great prophet, without whose advice his chief would do nothing. If he told the chief to pray, the people were called, and the sacrifices offered. If he foretold smallpox, nothing could avert it, except prayer and repentance. When he foretold war, the people got ready for fight or flight as he advised. He was unlike all other men. Biting ants left him alone; bees never stung him; snakes cleared from his path. Every one admired him. From birth to death his hair was never cut, and no word of his ever fell to the ground. To this day the people protect their houses from biting ants by sprinkling earth from his grave all around, and no ant will pass that sacred barrier, for Ntindi is their lord.

Such stories are very numerous. How did they arise? It may be a vain inquiry; but at any rate they are more than mere words; they witness to something lying deep in the native mind. Were the people, or some of them, convinced that life is bigger potentially than it is in actual fact? and did they invent these stories to satisfy a craving for redemption from the commonplace? Or did they believe that there is power available for certain persons, which is denied to common men? Perhaps uncommon incidents did occur, which were worked up into their present form by unconscious literary genius. It may be that we have here the dim beginnings of great works of imagination, or early forecasts of control over Nature by other forces than those of mere magic. " Trailing clouds of glory " behind them, these men have vanished from the daily life of the Konde ; but they went with a reputation that not even the greater glory of the white man has been able wholly to overshadow.

Index

The Mayflower Press, Plymouth   William Brendon and Son, Ltd.
1925